TRAMPING IN ARRAN

BY

TOM S. HALL

Author of

"TRAMPING HOLIDAYS IN SCOTLAND,"

ETC., ETC.

FALKIRK

THE WAYFARING ASSOCIATION

Tramping in Arran

This reprint published 2002

The Banton Press
Isle of Arran
Scotland.

ISBN: 1 85652 173 7

First Edition - - 1928
Second Edition (revised) 1938
Third Edition (revised) 1947

PRINTED IN GREAT BRITAIN BY
OLIVER AND BOYD LTD., EDINBURGH

CONTENTS

ILLUSTRATIONS

MAPS

PREFACE TO THIRD EDITION

IN the main, the third edition remains very much the same as the second edition, but with a few additions. The copy of the original mountain indicator chart is again included as well as the place name map. The Glen Ormidale excursion is new to *Tramping in Arran* and first appeared in the *Evening Citizen*, Glasgow, some years ago. It is included in the third edition by kind permission of the Editor of *The Citizen*. The Cir Mhòr walk and the visit to "The Hill of Birds' Nests" were originally published in "Tramping Holidays in Scotland" (*Country Life*), but in the new edition of that book the chapter on Arran has been omitted and the two excursions referred to have been included in the third edition of *Tramping in Arran*. I take this opportunity of thanking Mr Robert M. Gall Inglis for his helpful co-operation.

Also I thank the staff of the Reference Library, Dundee, for their valuable assistance.

Any reader who wishes to obtain further information or advice regarding a holiday in Arran should write to me and I will do what I can. I shall be very pleased to receive accounts of tramping holidays in Arran and suggestions for improving or altering the excursions given in this book.

TOM S. HALL.

4 HEUGH STREET,
FALKIRK, STIRLINGSHIRE.

MAP OF ARRAN

Port Fada
Cock of Arran
Newton
Loch Ranza
Hotel
Lochranza
Catacol Bay
Craw
Leniemore
(N. Thundergay)
S. Thundergay
Beinn Bhreac
Beinn Tarsuinn
Caisteal Abhail
Cioch-na h-Oighe
Cir Mhor
L. Tanna
Beinn Bharrain
Pirnmill
Imacher
Balliekine
Dougrie
Pier
Auchencar
Goat Fell
Beinn Tarsuinn
Glen Rosa
Brodick
Brodick Bay
Merkland P.
An Tunna
A R R A N
Machrie
Machrie Bay
Tormore
King's Caves
Ard Bheinn
Beinn Bhreac
Ballymichael
Shiskine
Shedog Inn
Glen Cloy
Corrygills
Claveland's Farm
Lamlash
Lamlash Bay
Blackwater Foot
Drumadoon Bay
Kilpatrick
Brown Head
Corriecravie
Castle Hills
Sliddery
Kiscadale
Ashdale
Whiting Bay
Dippin
Kilmory
Lagg Inn
Bennan Hd.
Kildonan Cas.
Pladda
Hotel
Corrie
North Sannox
Sannox Bay
Fallen Rocks
Glen Sannox
Glen Chalmadale
Kilbrennan Sound
Miles

INTRODUCING ARRAN

So brilliant was the landward view,
The ocean so serene,
  Each puny wave in diamond rolled
O'er the calm deep, where hues of gold
With azure strove and green
. . . .
Such was the enchanting scene.

—*The Lord of the Isles.*

SUCH is the enchanting scene as the traveller sails into the West from Ardrossan pier across to Brodick Bay. Approaching ever nearer is the island which will be your home for the next week or fortnight, and, no matter how you intend spending your leisure, Arran will readily cater for you. The geologist may spend many happy days among the hills and glens, just as Bryce did. His interest and attachment to the island can best be judged by his book entitled, *The Geology of Arran.* Landsborough, the botanist, loved the wildness of this island, and spent many holidays hunting for floral specimens. Those who wish to peep behind the curtain of the island's history and learn something of its folk lore should read *The East of Arran* and *Arran of the Bens, the Glens and the Brave.* Both these books are, of course, out of print, but copies can be obtained on loan from Public Libraries.

The Pioneer Glasgow tramper, Hugh Macdonald, described only one excursion to Arran, but, unforfortunately, his association was short. His books have been written for the most part for the botanist and for the geologist, and nothing so far has been written either by Macdonald or other writers exclusively for the tramper. Here, then, comes the opportunity of this book, but before proceeding with the excursions through the glens and over the bens, it is well that you should know something of Arran, both geographical and historical.

The Isle of Arran, in the Firth of Clyde, forms part of the county of Bute. It is situated in the mouth of the widening Firth, being separated by the Kilbrannan Sound from the peninsula of Kintyre, a distance of six miles. On the east is the Ayrshire coast, about thirteen miles distant. The Island of Bute, on the south, is five miles distant. The greatest length is from the Cock of Arran on the north to the Struey Rocks on the south, a distance of 26 miles; and the greatest breadth is 12 miles, from Clauchlands Point to Drumadoon Point. Its general shape is like a bean, indented in places by bays. The largest indentation is Lamlash Bay, which is bounded by Clauchlands Point and Kingscross Point, and sheltered by the Holy Isle. Loch Ranza, on the north-west, is the smallest bay, while Brodick has the finest situation.

The island is divided into two parishes; Kilbride on the east and Kilmory on the west, but it is topographically divided into five districts—Brodick, Lamlash, Southend, Shiskine and Lochranza. The north end of the island is composed of grim and towering peaks and deep wild glens, while the south end is rolling upland and pasture land. These peaks constitute the crowning glory of Arran, and are, perhaps, the main reason why so many people are attracted year after year.

There are three castles on the island Loch Ranza (in ruins), Kildonan (in ruins) and Brodick Castle. There was also a castle at Lamlash at one time, at Whitehouse, but practically all trace has now vanished.

The Arran roads are narrow, winding and interesting. The most important is that which follows the coast line right round the island, a distance of 56 miles. Some there are who like to boast that they have walked it in one day; many there are who have done it in two days, while the popular length of time for this undertaking is three days. I have not accomplished this feat, but I have walked from Catacol to Machrie and then hired a conveyance across to Brodick, from which place I walked back to Catacol by way of Corrie and Glen Chalmadale—all in the one day. Few roads cross the island. There is The String from Brodick to Machrie, and another road from Lamlash to Sliddery.

The early history of the island is very hazy and

almost unknown. Legend tells the story of how Fingal and his giants lived here, and there are the tales of the men of the Stone Age, who, it is said, lived in the wild glens, and by the shores. The Celts were early inhabitants, and were subdued by the Norwegians, who held the land until defeated at the Battle of Largs in 1265. In the early part of the fourteenth century, Bruce made history in the island, and then throughout the centuries, little is heard of Arran, except for Cromwell's men holding the Castle.

Brodick Castle is the only inhabited castle on the island, and is occupied by the owner of the estate. The history of this castle goes back many centuries. During the invasion of Haco, the castle was reduced by the Norwegians and was rebuilt by James, The High Steward of Scotland. Bruce took the castle by force from the English, and from the turrets watched for the beacon lights at Turnberry. From this date onward, the castle appeared to change hands often, and was often burned to the ground and rebuilt up to the time of the '45, when the castle and estate were possessed by the Duke of Hamilton. From that date onwards, the island was left in a state of tranquillity and nothing of historical import has since been enacted there.

In the eighteenth century, many improvements were introduced into the conditions of farming on the island. It is told that the tutors of the Duke of

Hamilton (a minor at the time) engaged a Mr John Birrell to effect improvements, "to reset the tacks, and to advise the measures to be adopted for improvement and to direct the operations resolved on." Mr Birrell effected many changes, some of which were the cause of many evictions from farms. About 500, mostly from Sannox, were sent to North America.

Pennant, in his book dealing with Arran, tells, that the people of Arran are hospitable to strangers, this is equally true at the present time, and, it can be said that they are a very warm-hearted people.

Arran alters little. Being entirely a "pleasure island" no smoking chimneys pollute the air. It is impossible for the railways to bring commercialism, and, although the motor-car has found its way there, the position of the island does not allow motor charabancs to come flocking from other places. The roads would be a nightmare if this state of affairs came to pass. Arran is unspoiled, and has been handed to us out of the pages of history without much alteration.

The country in the north of Arran is of such a type that the experienced tramper, armed with a one-inch map, should find it difficult to become lost. On the rolling uplands of the South, however, the way is not so easily found, but provided the mist does not descend, the sea is always there as a guide, and although you may not strike the path you hoped for, you will be sure of reaching some habitation ere long.

A good map is essential to the tramper, particularly

the leader of the party, and the one to be recommended for this district is the special map of Arran one inch to the mile, issued by the Ordnance Survey.

It is worth while quoting the remarks of R. L. S. regarding maps. He says, "I am told there are people who do not care for maps and find it hard to believe. The names, the shapes of the woodlands, the courses of the rivers and roads, the prehistoric footsteps of man still distinctly traceable uphill and down dale, the mills and the ruins, the ponds and the ferries, perhaps the standing stone of the Druidic Circle on the heath : here is an inexhaustible fund of interest for any man with eyes to see or twopence worth of imagination to understand with."

After a number of years of tramping, it is difficult to understand how one could go a-wandering without the precious map. There is another point which all walkers, particularly those who are new to the game, should bear in mind, that is the question of dress, and the most important item of dress is—boots. For the rough walking on Arran, boots are advisable, but, because of that, the inexperienced should not purchase a heavy pair of nailed boots just before the holiday, and feel that nothing more is required. Alas, this poor mortal would suffer agonies with chafed and blistered feet, and ere the first day was through would imagine the boots weighed a ton. Buy the boots with care ; low, sturdy and wide heels, soft leather uppers, and nailed in such a way that the nails do not come through inside the boot. After the purchase, keep them well oiled. " Walk them in " before the holiday, and by so doing you will not suffer any distress. Remember, too, that clean socks or stockings help to prevent blisters and soreness. When on tramp, always wear your oldest clothes. They are most serviceable and won't spoil. No need to worry then about bogs or water or rain or anything. Forget that collars and umbrellas ever existed, and if you must carry a hat, be sure to keep it in your pocket or rucksack all day. On second thoughts, an old battered hat is a real friend, it keeps the head dry ; it can be used as a drinking cup, is handy for fanning a fire and is useful as the top layer of a pillow. The best sort of hat is the one you have to rescue repeatedly from the church jumble sale.

Yonder in the heather, there's a bed for sleeping,
Drink for one athrist, ripe blackberries to eat,
Yonder in the sun, the merry hares go leaping,
And the pool, is clear for travel-wearied feet.

. . . .

Oh, my heart is fain to hear the soft wind blowing,
Soughing through the fir tops up on northern fells.
Oh, my eye's an ache to see the brown burn flowing
Through the peaty soil and tinkling heather bells.

—Ada Smith, *The Open Road.*

ARRAN'S MIGHTIEST WATERFALL

Whoever you are, come forth, or man or woman come forth.
You must not stay sleeping and dallying there in the house,
though you built it, or though it has been built for you.

—Walt Whitman.

Lamlash.—Route in brief. Glen Ashdale and Whiting Bay. Walking distance, 12 miles. The track is from Monamore Glen over the moors and down Glenashdale Burn to Whiting Bay. Return by main road or (a mile farther) by Kingscross Point and the shore.

THE two outstanding features of this excursion are (1) the almost limitless expanse of sea as viewed from the southern uplands of the island, and (2) the awe-inspiring wonder of the double fall of the Glen Ashdale waterfall, "where the burn draps in faem o'er the brown-breasted steep."

Commence this excursion by following the road through Lamlash, passing the old harbour. The *Imperial Gazetteer of Scotland* states, "Duchess Ann, who seems to have been a woman of superior capacity, caused a harbour to be built of large quadrangular blocks of sandstone. We may form some idea of the magnitude and solidity of this work when informed that it cost £2,913, 10s. 5d. sterling, at a time when masons' wages are said to have been 8d., and labourers' wages 4d. per day." "It is a great pity," says Headrick, "this building was allowed to be demolished. This harbour has now nearly disappeared; a great part of the stone having been carried off to build the new quay, a few hundred yards to the north, and the sand has buried a part." This "new quay" has now been superseded by the large wooden pier, but small vessels, such as coal lighters, still used the old pier. The reference to coal lighters brings to mind the problem of bringing coal to the island. It has been common custom for a small community on the island to co-operate and order a load of coal from the mainland. This is delivered by a lighter which steams to the locality and anchors at full tide as near inshore as possible. At low tide, the vessel is beached high and dry, when work commences with a will. Carts are backed to the side of the vessel and filled in a primitive manner from a basket operated by a windlass. If possible, the unloading is done before the next tide, and it is no uncommon sight to see the horses splashing through the rising water. In fact, the start is made before the boat is completely high and dry.

Passing through the village towards Whiting Bay, you come to the road junction at the Monamore Mill. At this point the route varies, according to the leader. Some will follow the Whiting Bay road for a short distance before striking on to the moorland, but my way is to follow up Monamore Glen for a short distance. A sparkling hill stream gurgles its course by the wayside, where the delicate bluebells nod their heads in May, and the brambles are juicy and sweet in early October.

On the left, the ramparts of the southern uplands rise to over 1,300 feet, and, as you have to scale these heights, you do well to study the contours. The ordnance map shows a path over these moorlands, right to Kilmory, but don't even try to find this path. Just make your own. This old road, now almost lost, is where the Giant Scorri met the women bringing their butter and eggs to Lamlash. The women, frightened at his awful appearance, dropped their wares and fled for dear life, whereupon the wily old giant gathered up the baskets and retired to his cave in Glen Scorradale to enjoy his feast at leisure. But the men of Arran eventually rose up against him and slew him in his own glen (see page 192 *East of Arran*), so you need have no fear that some fearsome monster will come and steal your rucksack!

Soon after the glen road starts climbing, you should take to the moorlands on the left, and follow one of the hill streams. You will observe how two streams are lined with trees; follow the burn on the right hand until you top the first rise.

The way is now less steep, as you are faced with long sloping uplands, culminating in the ridge beyond which is the plateau containing the eerie Urie Loch.

The Magic Hills—Brodick Bay at Sunset *E. W. Talle*

As you climb, make for the shoulder on the left of the ridge, and having topped this you should be in sight of the Urie Loch, a grey and lonely stretch of water cradled in a dimple of the moorlands. The meaning of the name Urie Loch is given by Rev. Duncan M'Nicol of Lochranza as the "Loch of the Yew Trees," whereas another writer gives it as the "Loch of the Brown Water." Both writers were considered authorities on the matter, but the meaning "Yew Trees" in a place so bleak and treeless seems inappropriate, while the meaning "Brown Water" seems a weak definition. However, we must leave it at that, content with the knowledge that there is so much of real interest in the ramble.

From the loch continue south until you obtain a view of the wide moorlands. Little more than a quarter of a mile away in a south-westerly direction you see Tighvein, 1497 feet, the highest point in the southern half of the island. Make this your next objective wading through the heather. What a view is everywhere unfolded! The mainland, partly screened in the haze of distance appears to mingle with the waters stretching from the nearby shores of the island. Lamlash and the Holy Isle are set out like a relief map and all around is a sea of heather. Across the moor in the direction of the Holy Island you will see the Loch na Leirg within the depths of which a great monster lived at one time. It had the skin of a seal and the bill of a sea goose, and was in the habit of attacking anyone who came too close. Once again, you need not be afraid, for the monster died many long years ago.

From the summit of Tighvein, you walk in a south-easterly direction, taking for your guide a post stuck on an eminence. Having reached this, you are looking down to Glen Ashdale. It is the one and only glen leading down to Whiting Bay, and you can quite easily follow its course from being just an impression on the moorland to where it becomes a deep ravine.

Having crossed the moorland to the Glenashdale Burn, you now traverse by its side a wonderful region Heather and bracken, sudden falls and unexpected bends in the gully, and then comes the crowning experience of the day—Glen Ashdale Falls. The path brings you to a platform at a point where the stream makes its first and awful plunge. Striking a ledge, the water leaps again into space to the bottom of the glen, far, far below.

The change from the quietness of the hills to the mad rush of the falls is indeed impressive. A few minutes ago you were walking by the side of the hill stream, whose waters whispered in the leisurely passing to the pebbles. Then the quietness is shattered and you stand enthralled with the noise and tumult of the waters leaping to the depths below.

On the high ground above this fall, the Longheads, a tribe of men who lived in the Stone Age, built their settlement, and buried their dead in the funeral cairns of Glen Ashdale.

This glorious glen is worthy of Switzerland. The deep sides of the gorge form a setting that is in full accord with the thunder of the fall. First, you should stand on the platform on the northern side, and then, retracing your steps, cross the stream above the fall and approach from the south side, where you can peep into its depths. For the next impression descend to the foot of the gorge and explore right to the black chasm where the water falls. There is a roar of thunder and a rhythmic swish of cascades of water dashing on the stones. The rocks round about have the blackness of night upon them, accentuating the white foam of the waters, touched here and there by the sun. All is dark around. Rocks lie glistening with a wet veneer of spray. Ferns hang from perilous rocks, and the deep, black pool is suggestive of night, even when the sun is at its brightest.

On either side of the glen, a path leads back to Whiting Bay. The south side path is high above the stream, while the north path hugs the burn. Both ways are muddy and dirty, but, after the moorland, you won't much care.

At Whiting Bay village, you have the choice of returning to Lamlash by steamer or motor, or you may walk by the road or Kingscross Point. The latter route would however be rather strenuous after the walking already done.

OVER THE MOORS FROM DRUMADOON

When the green woods laugh with the voice of joy,
And the dimpling stream runs laughing by,
When the air does laugh with our merry wit,
And the green hill laughs with the noise of it.

—Wm. Blake (1757-1827).

Route—West Coast, Drumadoon and King's Cave. Walking distance, 14 miles.

ONE evening, a party of us gathered for a "crack" about Arran.

"How did you enjoy the tramp over the hills to Drumadoon, Peggy?" I asked.

"It was grand."

"Which way did you go?"

"Up Monamore Glen and then over the moorland, but I couldn't tell you the route, because the mist came down and we were lost!"

Nevertheless it was "a grand walk" in spite of mist, but I won't describe such a walk as that, although it would bring many a reminiscent chuckle from my readers. It would be better to journey by motor to Blackwater Foot and describe the journey home from there over the hills to Lamlash.

The motor run from Lamlash to Blackwater Foot is full of interest and delight all the way. Through the village, and then up the road for Whiting Bay, where a commanding view of the Holy Isle is obtained. Then, after a backward glance at the peaks surrounding Goat Fell, you descend to Whiting Bay. Beyond the long, straggling street that constitutes the village, you continue to Dippin and so to Kildonan with its old ruined castle. In a dark recess in the vicinity of Dippin Head, there is said to be the entrance of a subterranean passage to the mainland, and it is also told (in a whisper, mark you !) that the plaintive howl of a dog and the distant skirl of the pibroch is heard o' nights by fishermen and others blessed (or cursed) with a grand imagination. Well, well, it is daylight as we pass, and the sun ought to be shining, so I doubt you will not hear the pipes. Of course, you might think you hear something resembling a piper, but be careful how you express your thoughts to the others.

You will see Pladda Island, off Kildonan, as you follow the south coast road to Sliddery, after which a final five miles of superb seascapes brings you to the little place of Blackwater Foot, which might aptly be called Backwater Foot.

The lazy part of the day is ended, but, ere starting on the more strenuous duties, an easy-going stroll is indulged in, just to bring the leg muscles into play. Drumadoon and the King's Caves are the immediate objective. The places are near at hand, and directions are unnecessary. If you wish, you can ask your way from the policeman on point duty !

The promontory of Drumadoon is the first place to

visit. Regarding the geology of the cliffs, Bryce says, "The porphyry of the cliff is in columnar forms, the pentagon being the prevailing figure, and there are irregular flat jointings; the pillars are from 1 to 2 feet on the side, and the height 80 or 100 feet at the middle or highest part of the precipice; the entire height being about 230 feet."

The rounded ridge of Drumadoon was at one time a fort and a sanctuary. Martin, in *Western Islands*, says: "of old it was a sanctuary, and whatever number of men or cattle could get within were secured from the assaults of enemies, the place being privileged by universal consent." Traces of the walls are still visible, and show that it must have been a place of great strength and capable of harbouring a large number of people.

"With a sufficient supply of water," says Headrick, "it might be rendered impregnable."

Drumadoon headland provides a wonderful range of colour and scenery in its wide, embracing view—a glorious stretch of sea in front, and rich fields of brown rolling uplands behind. Quite near is Shiskine, all spick and span, while at the foot of the rocks below, the Antlantic booms its continuous arrival.

From the promontory, a path leads down through the boulder-strewn beach of many ages ago to the King's Cave—the home of Fingal and the refuge of Bruce, as well as the meeting-place of smugglers. What tales those walls could tell—but they won't.

There is a story that a son was born to Fingal the Giant in this cave, and that this son is said to have left a footprint on the side of the cave, measuring more than 2 feet (linear) in length. If his build was in proportion to his feet, Mr Headrick has worked it out that the child was 70 or 80 feet high !—and it must be remembered that the child was only a day old when the impression was made. Now, assume that the proud father was four times the height of the child, Fingal *père* must have been over 300 feet high !

After landing at Loch Ranza, and prior to seizing Brodick Castle, the Royal Bruce is said to have resided in one of these caves. Possibly his fleet found shelter in Loch Ranza while he and his retinue found good lodging in the caves.

So many pens have described the formation, etc., of the caves that I will content myself by quoting from one of these only. Mackenzie MacBride says, "The roof is arched, and the place lofty and spacious, and on the walls are primitive drawings of dogs and horses engaged in the chase, probably dating from prehistoric times and, according to tradition, intended to represent Fion." The cave is 120 feet in length, 40 feet in breadth, and 50 feet high. One of the Drumadoon caves was used for many years by Mr Peter Craig as a school, turning out many good scholars.

Now we must turn our backs on these caves, once the home of Fingal, the camp of Bruce, and the stronghold of the smuggler. Many's the tale that the south coast of Arran could tell of fights with the excisemen. The duty was heavy on whisky, and, as a man must live, the whisky had to be made, and made it was, in many a wee clachan, and never a penny of duty paid.

If you will spread out your 1-inch map of Arran, we will trace out together the route to follow, because you are going to walk to Lamlash from Drumadoon—and not by The String road. First of all, find the King's Cave and then look for the Ross Hill, on the north side of the Monamore Glen road, between the seventh and eighth milestones. Draw a line between these two places, and you have the route you should take. What do you find along this line? There is the hill of Torr Righ Mòr, the highest point of the surrounding country. Then comes Shiskine and the Black Water, flowing out of the Clauchan Glen, a deserted place that leads to the hill lands and the Monamore Glen.

From the top of Torr Righ Mòr, you will see across the wide heath to the standing stones of Machrie Moor. Should you wish to visit these relics of long dead ages, descend the hill on the north side to the farmhouse of Tormore on the main road by the letter-box. Quite near the farm, a path going east leads to the ancient monoliths. Standing in a rude circle in the midst of this wide moorland, these stones present a majestic appearance. Bryce describes at great length the excavations he and his party made, the result of which was to open up an ancient sepulchre which

Arran Sky Line

F H. Do

The Castles and The Witch's Step

contained an urn—no doubt a funeral urn of some great chief. Further excavations followed, and the conclusion arrived at was that in reality these stone circles were cemeteries of some ancient community.

To the north of the circles, the Machrie burn flows to the sea. Follow this stream towards the hill as far as the woodlands, and then strike east over the moorlands, when you will come to the road. Turning south, you will have to walk a little over a mile before you come to the Black Water. If you have not visited the standing stones, you will cross the moor to the east from the top of Torr Righ Mòr.

By following this route, you will come to the Machrie-Blackwater Foot road, and, nearby the United Free Church, you turn to the left along the road going east to Shiskine. Crossing the Black Water, you come to the Brodick road, and by turning to the left, you pass through Shiskine village, and so to the bridge over the Black Water, where the road bends round sharply to the left. Hereabouts there are two old hill paths, leading over to the Sliddery Water. One path leads off the road by the church at Ballygown, and crosses the southern slopes of Beinn Tarsuinn and comes out on the Sliddery road by the bridge, about midway between the farms of Burican and Bennecarrigan. Maps of seventy or eighty years ago show this as a road, but it has long since lost the right to be called as such, and now it has difficulty in keeping up the name of a track. This is not your route, instead try to follow the other track that branches off the road along the Black Water at the bridge already mentioned. Going in an easterly direction, you follow the line of the stream, right up to and over the watershed. After a short distance, the path leads over the stream to lose itself at no great distance in an old quarry. You will lead on up the stream and follow the second tributary on the right. In this manner, you will lead over the watershed and will soon strike the head waters of Benlister Glen, which will bring you down to Lamlash through a wild, delightful coun'ry.

Although the greatest height achieved in this tramp is not more than 1,000 feet, you will find the day quite strenuous, because of the rough heather walking. Undoubtedly you will vote it a good day.

GOAT FELL, 2866 FEET

THE MOUNTAIN OF WIND

I've traversed many a mountain strand,
Abroad and in my native land,
And it has been my lot to tread
Where safety more than pleasure led ;
Thus many a waste I've wandered o'er,
Clombe many a crag, cross'd many a moor,
But, by my halidome,
A scene so rude, so wild as this,
Yet so sublime in barrenness,
Ne'er did my wandering footsteps press,
Where'er I happ'd to roam.

—*The Lord of the Isles*.

Route in Brief.—Motor to Brodick, thence take coast road round the bay and through the woods of Brodick Castle, by track to summit.

Descend round Meall Bheag and follow the stream to Corrie, walking back to Brodick by way of Merkland Point.

The round is approximately 12 miles.

THERE is the day's march set out for you in the baldest language. It is the walk for which you came to Arran. At Ardrossan pier, the hill called to you ; at Brodick pier, it mocked you ; and each day since, it has challenged you. To-day is the day.

It would be folly to estimate this tramp by the number of miles quoted. Twelve miles ? Why, such a distance by road is but a pleasant saunter, but the same distance over bog, rock and heather is an entirely different matter.

Some folks are inclined to think too great a stress is placed on the need for strong boots, but there is every need for this precaution. All those who have tried the game know what is wanted, but anyone who has never seen anything worse than a muddy lane on a stormy night has no conception. Boots are preferable to shoes, because of the added support to the ankles. It is a fallacy to think that you won't get your feet wet if you wear boots. You can be sure that if you go off the beaten track, you will finish up wet footed, no matter how you are shod.

I remember stepping into a bog in Glen Rosa and sinking up to my middle ! Even waders would have been useless then. In fact, nothing short of a diving suit can keep out the moisture. Recently I was tramping over Kinder Scout in Derbyshire, and the advice at the commencement of the tramp to the members of the party was to jump in the stream and deliberately immerse their feet. Mad, I know, but you would be surprised how much relieved in mind you will be. There is now no need to worry about getting your feet wet—they are wet. Those who are no longer young in mind will shake their heads over this, but let me quote from David Grayson for their benefit: "My sober friend, have you ever tried to do anything that the world at large considers not quite sane? Try it! It is easier to commit a crime!"

Now for the excursion. Assuming your headquarters are at Whiting Bay, the motor car will carry you to Brodick over the wonderful moorland road you will walk along as the introductory to the Clauchland Hills ramble. To-day, you speed over the same road at a great rate, but in lifting your eyes from things at hand, you may dwell upon the summit of Goat Fell—the hill of the winds.

Perhaps a fat white cloud is moving slowly to take a rest on the sharp summit, and perhaps upon landing, the delicate fabric of the cloud is pierced, allowing the rocks to peep through.

There are two definitions as to the meaning of Goat Fell. One informant says it is the Hill of the Goats, so named because of the goats that at one time grazed there. It is more likely that the name is a corruption of the Gaelic "Gaodh Bhein" or "Ben Ghaoil," meaning "The Hill of the Winds."

The commencement of the ascent is through the woods of Brodick Castle, and then on to the moorland, bogs and heather. Later on, nearer the top, the going is firmer, as you are on the bare rock, and then, finally, at the summit, you are in the midst of a wild chaotic tumble of rocks.

From Brodick, follow the Corrie road, skirting the golf course and the bay. About 300 yards beyond the

Standing Stone, which is almost facing the school, a path leads to the right across the stream to bring you to the road again, a little short of Brodick Castle stables, from which point the climb commences. Just before starting the climb, walk a little farther along the shore road to visit the little harbour for Brodick Castle. It was built in honour of King Edward VII.'s visit to the Castle.

From the Castle stables, the road through the policies leads to the kennels, and then the path ahead through further woodlands brings you to the edge of the moorlands. A stream on the left should be your guide for a short distance, and then a line of cairns marks the path up to the ridge. From the shore, this ridge looks quite smooth, but in reality it is a series of steps, each one of which consists of a steep rocky slope topped by a comparatively level platform. The last lap calls for more strenuous stuff ; you are in the midst of what has been called the Cyclopean Walls. At last you reach the summit and, if you are lucky, find a view of a lifetime awaiting. The summit would be perfect in every way if it possessed a spring of water. After the arduous climb and a rest, it is good to lounge there, seemingly on top of the world, and eat your lunch—but although there is no spring of water, you will find minute pools of water in little hollows of rock.

Goat Fell gives the impression of being the hub of the island, from which spokes radiate to different points of the compass. One ridge leads to the north-west down to The Saddle dividing Glens Sannox and Rosa. Beyond The Saddle this ridge loses its identity in the solid mass of Cir Mhòr, from whose summit a track leads to The Castles, where the clouds trail up like smoke from a chimney. Turning in the reverse direction, you see the bays of Brodick, Lamlash and Whiting Bay, and Holy Isle sits in close to the land as if to shelter the village. Out at sea "Paddy's Millstone"—Ailsa Craig—stands out clearly as the guardian of the Firth.

At one time, the only communication between Ailsa Craig and the mainland (at Girvan) was the pigeon post. These homing pigeons would fly to the home loft at Girvan and enter the loft by small swing doors which, by means of en electrical contact, would cause a bell to ring in the house. Communication was later maintained by wireless between island and mainland, but the pigeons were retained for emergency.

Look upon the climb as an adventure, being prepared to conquer no matter what comes. The first time I climbed Goat Fell was in 1922. My friend and myself spent the night in a bivouack in the woods above the Castle and then, the next morning, hiked across the shoulder of the hill until we were looking down on Corrie. We then dumped our kit in the heather and set our faces for the summit, but, alas, the mist caught us as we were scrambling up out of the Coire nam Meann to the ridge. We managed, however, to reach the top, where we stayed a moment or two shivering with the intense cold—but we had conquered and that was enough.

By the way, I left a small shaving mirror hanging on a tree at this one-night camp. Perhaps it is still hanging there. If it is and you should find it, do not bother to return it—I have another.

If the day is clear, a wonderful view is unfolded—an ideal place for a geography lesson. To the north-east, you see the two Cumbraes, and behind them, Largs, Wemyss Bay and the Clyde sparkling with white sails, and the hills of Renfrewshire in the background. To the north is Bute and the Kyles, while Ben Lomond, Ben Vorlich and Ben Ledi fill up the distant background. To the north-west, the eye reaches far up Loch Fyne, and round by the Paps of Jura and Islay and Mull. Looking across Beinn Nuis down to the Sound of Kilbrannan, you see Campbeltown and over Kintyre, and, if the day is particularly clear, the coast of Ireland. Due south, you see Wigtownshire and Ailsa Craig, with Pladda, the Holy Isle and Lamlash in the foreground. Looking east, the eye sweeps round the coast of Ayrshire, taking in Ayr, Troon, Irvine and Ardrossan, and inland the conical Loudon Hill. East and south-east are the Muirkirk and Cumnock ranges, Cairnsmuir, and the dark mountains between Loch Doon and Loch Trool, several of which are nearly as high as Goat Fell.

Another writer describes the scene as "the most terrible congregation of jagged mountain ridges to be seen anywhere in the same compass, and yawning chasms between—all grey, bleak and barren in the extreme." I will not add to that.

If suitable, lunch is taken on the top, and those who are new to the game should remember to collect any litter. Always remember this whenever out picknicing. If everybody did this, more beauty spots would be open to the public.

The descent is to Corrie, which lies, roughly speaking, in a line east of the summit. You climbed up to the summit from the south, but in your descent, you should climb down into the Coire nam Meann, which is that deep recess on the east side of Goat Fell. After negotiating the steep boulders into this gully, continue out through the wide mouth on to the open moorlands, and by following an easterly direction, you should have no difficulty in finding Corrie. Provided the atmosphere is good, it will be comparatively easy to decide your direction. The glens are so deep and well defined that, with the help of your map, you can easily see which is the Coire nam Meann.

The final part of the walk is by the shore road to Brodick and then by motor home. Seated at dinner, you feel the glow of the moorland wind on your face, and feel that your evening prayer should end—

"And every eve I say,
Noting my step in bliss,
That I have known no day,
In all my life like this."

The Goat Fell Mountain View Indicator.

The Story of its Inception.

The idea was first discussed at a meeting of the Arran Ceilidh in Glasgow in 1928. At that time the indicator for Ben Lomond was in course of construction, and, following the completion of this work, attention was directed to Arran. *The Daily Record*, as in the case of the Ben Lomond erection, again readily agreed to gift the indicator to the public, provided the erection work would be undertaken by the inhabitants of Arran. The Publicity Committee of Arran promised to supply the labour, and they in turn arranged with Brodick Improvement Trust to take the matter in hand. Finally, the late Mr Hendry, of Brodick, took charge, and he, with his band of voluntary workers, saw the task to completion as soon as the necessary permission had been given by Her Grace the Duchess of Montrose.

Time Table of Events.

King's Birthday, 1929 :

Visit to the summit to choose a site.

July 7th and July 14th :

Ascent of work parties for erection of cairn.

July 20th :

Top plate fixed by compass bearing. Magnetic variation for Goat Fell, 1929, 17° 15′ W.

August 4th :

Erection work completed.

August 9th :

Chart placed in position in readiness for opening ceremony.

August 10th :

Opening ceremony at the summit.

During the investigations, many interesting points pressnted themselves. Of all the peaks that are visible, not one is over 4,000 feet, and 11 only are more than 3,000. According to the chart, it is possible to see 122 peaks, 16 of which are higher than Goat Fell. The greatest distances are Ben More in Mull (63½ miles) to Skiddaw in the Lake District (105 miles) and from Slieve Snought in County Donegal (89½ miles) to Ben Lawers (74 miles).

The greatest array of mountains are in the north to north-east, where nine of the peaks over 3,000 feet are to be found. Ben Lomond is the sixth highest peak to be seen ; also it was decided quite definitely that Ben Nevis is not visible.

The chart was drawn by Mr D. K. Paterson of Paisley, who has done very good work in preparing similar charts for a number of view points in Scotland. Mr Hendry, of Brodick Publicity Committee, and a band of local workers were responsible for the erection work. About five hundredweights of cement were used, and water from the natural reservoirs in the rock hollows was utilised by the mixers. The use of water from these small reservoirs was the result of a discovery made at the time by a party of fellows from the 5th Glasgow B.B. They arrived at the summit, hot and drouthy, and the sight of drier sandwiches set the party scouting for water.

After the cairn had been erected, the iron table was placed in position and set by compass and allowance made for the magnetic variation.

This was calculated to the wrong side of north, and the cairn had to be partly rebuilt to rectify this. What an outcry if Ben Lomond was shown as being somewhere in Mull!

The chart was placed in position on the morning of the ceremony, and the lot fell upon my shoulders to carry the sheet of glass to the summit. It was carried in an aluminium sling and strapped securely to my back. We reached the summit in safety, but, in screwing down the frame, the glass cracked.

What a calamity! and the ceremony only a few hours later. We hurried down the mountain—literally ran, and made a bee line for the glazier in the village.

"Have you a sheet of heavy glass, two feet four square?" said we as one, breathlessly. "Yes," was the answer, "I have just one piece of glass of the weight you will require."

With a thankful heart, we had lunch, and then back for the glass. He brought it from the workshop, but looking at the pane, I said doubtfully, "Is that 2 feet 4 inches square ?"

"Man, ye said 24 inches square !" And he had no more suitable glass in stock.

We made our second ascent that day with the crowd. About 300 enthusiasts climbed in the rain and mist, and, while waiting at the summit for the official party, songs were sung with great gusto. The party consisted mostly of ladies, and the journey was undertaken in 1¾ hours. His Grace the Duke of Montrose and his son, Lord Ronald Graham, attended the ceremony. Mr Rosslyn Mitchell handed over the Indicator to the people of Arran, and Lord Ronald Graham accepted the gift from the newspaper on behalf of the islanders.

The descent was made in thick mist and drenching rain. So thick was the mist that the Duke of Montrose and his son stood at one point on the hill-side to keep people on the right track.

At the suggestion of His Grace, the ceremony ended by singing *Auld Lang Syne.* All linked hands round the Indicator, and both the Duke and his son shared in the demonstration as heartily as any.

In all, 41 volunteers, mostly from Brodick, assisted in the erection work.

This and other mountain view indicators seem to be the particular object of abuse by certain types of people. These indicators are favourite places on which to carve initials, even to scratching initials on the glass. Not long after the erection of the first chart on Goat Fell some thoughtless person cracked the glass by using the top as a vaulting horse.

There have been a number of arguments from time to time as to whether it is possible, given the right visibility to see Ben Nevis from the summit of Goat Fell. The answer is No. As already stated not one of the peaks over 4,000 feet can be seen. In fact, the possibility of seeing Ben Nevis was checked very carefully and it was shown then that it is not possible to see the Ben. Another point that requires to be cleared up is whether all the heights shown on the chart can be seen. The answer in this case is YES. Every height shewn can be seen given the right visibility.

Shortly after the war it was ascertained by a visit to the sumit that the indicator pedestal was in fairly good order and would require little attention. The chart was of course not in position but it was held in safe custody in a house in Glen Rosa. Plans were made to have the chart placed in position but it was decided to wait until the next summer before undertaking the work. It is expected therefore that by the time this edition is published the chart will once more be in position. All those visiting the summit are asked not to use the indicator as a visitors book. It is not really necessary to leave your name and address or to send the world your greetings etc.

THE HOLY ISLE

"Through scenes where brightest beauty smiles."

HOLY ISLAND gains its name from being the hermitage of one of the earliest Christian missionaries in Scotland—St. Molios. Born in A.D. 566, he retired at the age of 20 to the island which was called "Isle-a-Molass" or Lamlash Isle. There are inscriptions in Runic letters on the roof of the cave where he is said to have lived, but these have no reference to Molios. The words "Nicolas hann raisti" (Nicolas this engraved) are said to be Norse, and probably refer to a Norwegian hermit who dwelt here when the Northerners ruled the Western Isles about 1100 A.D. (see Bryce's *Arran*, page 136). The route to the island is as described by Boyd Scott in *East of Arran*. He sails from Lamlash old pier—so will you. He lands on the island at the little quay below the farm, and so will you. Continuing his narrative, he tells us that in leaving Lamlash, we have left what is not Lamlash at all, and on reaching the Holy Isle, we have really reached Lamlash. In days long past, when St Molios and his disciples lived on the island, the mainland opposite was inhabited by only a small colony in rude huts. The island was of more importance, and was known as Eilan Moloise (Isle of St Molios), and through time the name developed to Lan Moloise, Lawmolach, and so Lamlash—a name later applied to the cluster of habitations on the mainland.

The Holy Isle is 1¾ miles in length, and from 3¾ to 5 furlongs in breadth. It is of igneous origin, the rock varying from claystone to compact felspar or clinkstone. This rocky mass rises from the sea in the shape of an irregular cone to a height of over 1,000 feet. There are two summits; the lesser being Mullach Beag (763 feet), and the greater, Mullach Mor (1,030 feet). From either of these commanding viewpoints, a magnificent panorama of the widening Firth is obtained.

> " . . . I love thee, gentle Clyde,
> For aye, as with a spell,
> Thou bring'st me back the cherished forms
> In mem'ry's haunts to dwell.
> Like sunshine on the distant hills,
> Life's early joys I see;
> And from the brightness of the past
> I dream what heaven would be."

Lamlash Bay is immediately below, and on a bright day, when the sea loch is crowded with shipping, the sight is indeed charming. What an impressive view of the Arran peaks is permitted. They stand out in true majesty—a ragged, rugged skyline. Having scaled some of these heights, you wonder how you managed to retain your hold on such dizzy precipices. The black summit of Cir Mhòr stands out clean-cut against the sky.

To return to the landing-stage once more. Nearby is the farm, the only habitation apart from the lighthouse at the southern extremity, which is connected to the farm by a path.

Goat Fell Pinnacles

The Witch's Step from Cir Mhòr

Andrew C. Gray

Walking this way, you are treading romantic and historic ground. The stories of St Molios are many and varied, according to the different writers. Bryce tells us the story given at the commencement of this chapter, and goes so far as to say it is the correct story. Then you read in the *Book of Arran* that the Runic characters on the wall of the saint's cave do not refer to Nicolas, a priest of Argyll, but " to a prosaic Norse trader, one Uilaeikr Stallr, which would appear to have as much meaning as " Bill Stumps—His Mark." Antiquaries are greatly at variance in accounting for the legend, and one irreverent investigator has suggested that the particular " Nicolas " must have been Auld Nick—the devil himself !—the inscription having been effected while the hermit slept !

The traces of a small cell or monastery, erected apparently in connection with the hermitage by Reginald de Insulis, between 1206 and 1212, and which was in ruins when visited in 1506 by Munro, Dean of the Isles, were till lately to be seen north of the cave. Here, also was a burying-ground, long used as the chief place of interment for Arran, till the loss of life by the upsetting of a boat. The funeral boat was swamped and several persons were drowned. After that, the present burial ground of Lamlash was sought out, to which it is said the people were guided by a light which appeared and led them on.

Close to the cave is a spring of pure water—the Saint's Spring—held in high repute for many centuries by the superstitious for its supposed healing qualities.

The folk lore of Arran contains many strange superstitious beliefs.

Measles and whooping cough would be cured if the patient drank sips of, and was sprinkled with, rain which has been caught in a saucer-shaped stone at a place where the sea was not visible.

There is the well-known superstition that a potato carried in the pocket would keep away rheumatism—by the way, potatoes have carried the name of the island far and wide. Who has not heard of the "Arran Banner" and "Arran Chief"—potatoes which were given to the world by Mr M'Kelvie of Lamlash?

To borrow salt during Christmas week was sure to bring sorrow; fishermen on the way to their boats would not sail if they met a flat-footed or dark-complexioned man; to allow the fire to go out would bring misfortune, and the same would apply if a kindling was given from the fire to another.

Bad luck would follow if a mother visited you before her child was baptised.

Flat-footed or fair-haired men are not allowed to first-foot at New Year—but that applies throughout Scotland at the present time.

So much, then, for history and legend.

A group of us once made history on the Holy Island. Here we held a rehearsal for a concert to be given in the local Navy Hall. The concert was in aid of the local hospital and was advertised throughout the island. It was expected that about half the Hall would be needed, but every inch of space in the Hall was filled. In fact, the approach to the Hall just before the concert started was more like the road to a football match. The artists were all guests from the Holiday Fellowship Guest House. I remember the event only too well, because I was chairman of the affair.

I like to look back on the Holy Island excursion as a lazy day. The ships riding at anchor in the bay, spelt laziness to me. I thought of the strenuous days on the crags and peaks and—and I gave in to my laziness. I lingered by the water's edge. I slept a little after the picnic lunch, and, later, sat skimming pebbles over the shining sea.

"What is this life if full of care,
We have no time to stand and stare,
No time to stand beneath the boughs
And stare as long as sheep and cows."

Eventually you must leave the island and once more walk the high road of New Lamlash.

THE FAERIE HILLS

" Crags, knolls and mounds, confusedly hurled,
The fragments of an earlier world
And mountains, that like giants stand,
To sentinel enchanted land."

Route in Brief.—Lamlash, Monamore Glen and Glen Cloy. Total walking distance, 10 miles. Through the glen and over the moors to Brisderg, thence down Glen Dubh, passing the mounds believed to be the remains of Bruce's Castle, following stream to Brodick. Return by old road to Lamlash. Return can be made by steamer by those who wish to do so.

THERE is a wild piece of country bounded by The String road, the Lamlash-Brodick road, and the Monamore Glen road, and it is my purpose on this excursion to conduct you across these wilds, right through the Faerie Hills. The Sheeans, as these Faerie heights are called on the map, guard the upper end of Glen Cloy, or, to be correct, Gleann Dubh (the black glen), and share the responsibility with another height nearby, called the Crag of the Raven. What a wonderful and wild playground for the faries this must be, but I think these little folk come up here on special occasions when they wish to dance to the wind. At other times, I think they would not wander so far from what must have been their home—Tornanshiain

—in the sheltered Glen Cloy. If you refer to your map, you will see a spot marked "Fort: Bruce's Castle." This marks the site of the faeries' mound where they live to this very day, as far as I know. Nowadays we do not hear so much of their doings, but past generations tell many a tale about them—and they were not all good ones, either. I am told, in fact, that they were a motley crowd. There were Pookas that took the shape of horses, and Giants and Bogles (or Bogies) and Bleaters, and another single fairy called the Hungry One. "The Bleater" must have been a nice kind of creature—"a thin grey woman" who came from nowhere in particular, and supposed to be the child of a mortal who had married a fairy. The Bocans haunt the burns and bridges (I think these must be the people who place bogs for you to step in).

To dream of a bird was very significant according to one old Arran superstition and was considered to be the prelude to some important domestic or clan event. Each clan or family had its own animal. For example, the cat was supposed to represent the MacNeishes and the goose the Fullartons, and so on. Let me be away on the tramp and not lingering over such eerie subjects.

As you start on your way, you pass the old schoolhouse of Lamlash. The stones for this building were taken from the chambered cairn on the farm of Blairmore, near the base of Dun Fionn. The breaking up of this cairn brings to mind that story of the farmer at Torlin, who rifled the cells of one of these cairns and strewed the bones over the field. The story goes on to say that "with daring irreverence, he selected one of the largest skulls from the ghastly heap and carried it home with him; but scarcely had he entered his house when its walls were shaken as if struck by a tornado. Again and again the avenging blast swept over his dwelling, though not a sign of the gentlest breeze was heard in the neighbouring wood. The affrighted victim hastened to rebury the bones in their desecrated grave, but day and night, shadowy phantoms continued to haunt his mind and track his steps, and, a few months after the commission of his rash deed, whilst riding along the highroad towards Lagg, he was thrown from his horse over a steep embankment, and dashed against the rocks of the stream beneath." It would appear that this tradition was well known in Arran, and tended to deepen the feelings of superstitious dread with which these monuments are regarded.

Follow the road to Monamore Mill, and on up the Glen road. On the left, the green ramparts culminate in the Squiler, and, on the right, The Ross squats down between Benlister and Monamore. In summer, this road is trying to the best of walkers, owing to its closeness, due to the confined nature of the glen. The road rises steeply, and ere long you have reached a point nearly level with the summit of The Ross.

Here you will strike north across the moorland, making your objective the hill of Brisderg.

So far, I have described the route originally followed, but now I am going to retrace my steps and take you a way that I think is better. Perhaps other leaders have taken the route I have chosen, because of the oppressive nature of Monamore Glen. Recently I was up this way to the top of the road, but I can frankly say I did not enjoy it, and all because of the enervating effect of the atmosphere.

This is the route, therefore, that I suggest. Turn up the Benlister Glen near Hamilton Terrace in the village, and follow the tree-lined way to Benlister clachan. You have the Ross Hill on your left now, as you follow the Benlister burn up to the hills. A farther mile of walking brings you to the junction of the Benlister burn and the Tounie, the former stream being on the left, and the latter on the right of the Tounie Hill. You may follow either stream, according to your inclinations. The left fork will lead you to another fork in the mountain stream, when, by following the right-hand course, you can lead on to the summit of Brisderg (1,332 feet). From this height, you must cross the moorlands slightly north-east to the Faerie Hills, which can now be seen plainly.

If you follow the Tounie burn to the right of Tounie Hill, you come by a shorter route to the Faerie Hills. Step by step, you trace out the stream to its source, when you are under the shelter of the Sheeans. During the morning, the view has been restricted to surrounding moorlands, but now the view is mighty and majestic. At your feet, the ground falls away abruptly into the Black Glen which, in turn, merges into Glen Cloy. On the left of the Glen, you see Glen Ormidale opening out, guarded to the north by the long ridge of Muileann Gaoithe. Then beyond all this is the wonderful jaggy outline of the island peaks. The Tower of Death (Caisteal Abhail) is smoking with clouds, as if the de'il and his satellites were mixing some unholy brew in the Devil's Punchbowl. Of the many views in the island, this is perhaps one of the finest, no doubt because of the suddenness with which it springs upon the vision. For some distance the track has been leading up to the heights and giving no hint of what is to come, and then, in a matter of a few minutes, the whole panorama bursts into view.

Here you should rest and partake of lunch. The sandwiches will taste better because of the long climb, and the lack of a cup of tea will be more than made up by the joy of the view. I remember when in the vicinity of the Sheeans, when poking about after lunch, that I made two discoveries. First, I found a nest in the heather, containing four brown speckled eggs, nestling in the softest down from the mother bird, and then in another place I found a fox's lair, which contained the remains of a lamb, while all around was strewn the wool of the carcase. What a gruesome contrast to the first discovery!

Over the Tops

The descent down the steep hill into Glen Cloy is a good scramble, where strong boots with serviceable heels are essential. I was surprised to read that Dr Landsborough recommends shoes for tramps, and, emphatically, I disagree. Boots are a necessary safeguard against a twisted ankle, a calamity that is a very serious matter when far from roads and houses.

Down in the glen, you will follow the stream, and by so doing, you will pass by the site of Bruce's Castle. Here it was that Bruce's advance guard stayed, after the successful attack on Brodick Castle. This gallant party had sailed from the island of Rathlinn, off the coast of Ireland, and landed at Lochranza. Crossing to the east of the island, the party attacked a number of soldiers unloading provisions at the boats. After killing most of the party, Bruce's men retired to the castle in Glen Cloy to rejoice in their early success. Here it was they were joined later by Bruce himself.

The meeting of Bruce is told by Barbour :

> The King then blew his horn on high
> And girt his men that were him by
> Hold them still and all privy
> And syne again his horn blew he ;
> James of Douglas heard him blaw
> And at last alane gane know
> And said, " Soothly, yon's the King."

Shortly after this gathering in Arran, Bruce crossed to Ayrshire, and ere long his forces were mustered at Tor Wood, in readiness for Bannockburn.

As already mentioned, M'Arthur, in his *Antiquities of Arran*, tells us that the site of Bruce's castle is known as the Faery Mound, but Boyd Scott, in his *East of Arran*, says that the name in Gaelic means the "Hill of the Old Fort," and that it is not likely Bruce built it. Posisbly the building was erected as a defence against the rovers of the sea, or by the rovers themselves, to consolidate what they had won so hardly.

Your path will lead you down to Invercloy, and so to the village of Brodick. The day has not been too strenuous, and there is no reason why you should not walk back to Lamlash by way of Strathwhillan and Dun Fionn. By doing this, you have completed the circle entirely on foot. In the morning, you left Lamlash by the south, and in the evening entered from the opposite direction. Returning to the house, is it not well to think of that verse from *The Hymn of Empedocles* ?

"Is it so small a thing
  To have enjoyed the sun,
To have lived light in the spring,
To have loved, to have thought, to have done ;
To have advanced true friends, . . ."

THE SOUTHERN UPLANDS

"Come, I will take you to the windy lands
Where twisted roans flame, and scarred rocks frown
In strong defiance; where hill-tarns are brown
And deep with shadowy dreams; where Beauty stands
Poised for mid-flight, grey-eyed with eager strands
Of hair stretched on the wind. We'll fling us down
Far from the hideous chimneys of the town,
And lie idle, with contemplative hands."

—G. A. Renshaw.

Route in Brief.—Across the moorlands from Lamlash to Kilmory.

THE Ordnance Survey map shows a path where once there was a road, while the moorland itself shows little trace of any path whatever. Climbing the hill to the Urie Loch for the first time, the tramper will look in vain for a path, unless by lucky chance he strikes a portion of the grass-grown roadway, and even then he may not recognise it as the old highway. The disuse of these old drove roads is not uncommon in Scotland. This applies also to the country within a wide radius of Glasgow, where many of these old ways can be traced though fast sinking back into the bog of the moorland. So with this road. In days past, it would, no doubt, be quicker to journey from Lamlash to Kilmory by this hill road rather than the coast route, although the same stiff gradient would not be encoutered on the latter course. Then, with the introduction of faster moving traffic, this hill road would fall into disuse and so, by degrees, vanish entirely. For the sake of those who love the moorlands and wild places, it is a pity that these rights of way should be lost.

The route to be following at the commencement of this tramp is the same as the excursion to Glen Ashdale, but only as far as the Urie Loch, or, perhaps, as far as the summit of Tighvein.

You walk a little way up Monamore Glen from Lamlash, and climb the hillside on the left, after which you come in sight of the Urie Loch. From there, continuing south, you soon reach Tighvein. From this high point, you survey the wide expanse of moorlands and the greater part of the south end of the island. Just which way to go now for Kilmory is not so easily decided, so it will be advisable to follow the instructions carefully.

Almost due south, about three-quarters of a mile distant, is a lesser hill, Glas Choirein (1,327 feet); make this your objective, and then continue a little way down the hill, still keeping due south. At a point somewhere on the 900 feet contour level, you should come to the Auchareoch Burn. Be quite sure you keep south and not south-west, or you may strike the stream feeding the Ashdale Water. However, the moorland permits a wide view of the Ashdale Glen, so you should not go wrong. Once having found the Auchareoch Burn, you are safe, as you follow the stream down to the farm of that name, whence a better defined track leads on.

The leader doing this walk for the first time, should work by land-marks. The first objective should be the Urie Loch, which is not difficult to attain. Next, climb out of the basin which holds the loch, and to the south, you will see Tighvein, easily distinguished because it is the highest point in the district. Then face south, when you see a post stuck upon a slightly lesser height, about three-quarters of a mile away. From there, your fourth objective is the Auchareoch Water below the hill-top. If, therefore, you do the tramp in the stages as suggested, you should have no fear of arriving at the Auchareoch Farm late for lunch.

And what of the view ? Truly it is wonderful.

The island of Pladda is near at hand, and, farther distant across the shining sea, furrowed into countless lanes by the wind, is Ailsa Craig, the bird sanctuary—Paddy's Milestone—the island that symbolises home to the returning Scot just as the Statue of Liberty does to the American.

The Mull of Kintyre and Davaar Island appear over to the west, while all around, the heather-clad moorlands sweep down to the sea.

Crossing through fairly broken country, the path from Auchareoch skirts to the east of the "Little Black Hill," then continues along the slopes of the valley holding Kilmory Water, and so down to the rather bleak place of Kilmory. Here is the end of this fine moorland walk, but there is the long and interesting motor drive yet to come—the drive back to Lamlash.

The scenery of this district is of a milder type than that of any other part of the island. The two main rivulets in this district are the Torryglen and the Sliddery. These and their tributaries have cut deep chasms in the strata, sometimes composed of large veins of whinstone interspersed with innumerable particles of pyrites, which retain their brilliancy in spite of exposure to the air. "These," says Headrick, "the people are confident in the belief of being gold; and I confess I was a little staggered, until my ingenious friend, Dr Thomson, by analysing a specimen, assured me that the gold was neither more nor less than pyrites of iron."

The motor run home from Kilmory is by way of Kildonan. Near by is Bennan Head and the famous Black Cave, the largest cave in Arran. Up to quite recent times, it was used as a preaching cave, and, away back in the Stone Age, may have housed the "arrow maker" whose rude instruments of stone and flint have been found both within the cave and buried in the moorlands of the island. Across from Bennan Head is Pladda Island, where a lighthouse stands to guide the mariner. This lighthouse, superseding the one of 1800, was built in 1826 to the designs of Robert Stevenson by Mr Broom, a contractor of Glasgow.

The next place of interest along the coast is Kildonan Castle, perched at the edge of the cliff and lifting its hoary head to the winds of heaven.

The castle is meagre in historical interest, but there is a legend of this old keep that is worth repeating. I read it in Brotchie's *Scottish Western Holiday Haunts*, and I pass it on to you as he gives it. "It may be recalled that, within the old grey keep of Kildonan, the last Barclay Baron of Ardrossan, known as the "De'il of Ardrossan," ended his wretched days. He it was who set his satanic majesty to erect a bridge from Cumbrae to the mainland, but as it was approaching completion, some luckless stranger happening to mention the Divinity, immediately Satan vanished in a flame of fire, overwhelming the bridge, but leaving the foundations, which may be seen to this day, one on the Cumbrae and the other near West Kilbride. Barclay retired afterwards to Kildonan."

Along the coast from Kildonan, you come to Dippen (The Twopenny Glen), said to be the other end of the Giant's Causeway, and possibly the place where Fingal the Giant stepped ashore. Passing Largybeg Point, you see the Holy Island together with the gentle bay of Kiscadale, or as it is more commonly known, Whiting Bay. Dr Landsborough tells of how in his boyhood days he saw a whale in the bay. This has not been an experience of mine in Arran, nor do I wish that it should be, after the boyhood recollections of the whale that was left high and dry on Blackpool sands. I shall never forget the terrible smell the carcase gave off. I like to think of Whiting Bay in its connection with Bruce. Other books tell of his coming to Arran and living in the fort in Glen Cloy. On this excursion, the route passes near the spot where the King sailed for Turnberry. This was at Kingscross. Interesting as this may be, it is not half so fascinating as the knowledge that the "Bruce and the spider" incident is said to have been enacted near Kingscross Point. As a boy I always loved that story, and, in my childish brain, I pictured a bearded King sitting watching the spider. Now, I can add the natural setting to this older mental picture, and, because of that, the tradition holds greater attraction. One writer has stated that the spider incident happened when the King was in hiding on the island of Rathlinn, but, according to other writers, Whiting Bay is associated with the legend.

This excursion covers a wider area than the tramp to Glen Ashdale, but in both cases the day finishes on the same route. On both occasions, there is the joy of travelling the highroad from Whiting Bay to Lamlash in the glow of the evening.

THE SADDLE
GLEN SANNOX AND GLEN ROSA

"I am tired of all the tame complacencies,
The comfortable dirt, the useless words.
I want the heights with you, the beating rain
On dwindling tracks, the pines like moaning seas,
Silence and Space, the wild dawn-song of birds."

Route in Brief.—Glen Sannox and Glen Rosa. Walking distance, 11 miles. This is a fairly hard day. Motor to Sannox Bay, thence track through the Glen, and, skirting the peak Cir Mhòr, follow the stream down Glen Rosa. Those who cannot do this round should walk back to Brodick by the shore road through Corrie, 7 miles. Return to Lamlash by motor if necessary.

THERE is no need to go into detail over the alternative route, *i.e.*, the walk by the shore to Brodick, as I shall describe that in the trip round the island. To-day's is a stern walk, so let us be away for—

"The wonderful air is over me
And the wonderful wind is shaking the tree;
It walks on the water and whirls the mills,
And talks to itself on the tops of the hills."

You will alight from the motor at Sannox Bay, where the path leaves the road by the tea-room. The word Sannox is said to be a corruption of the Gaelic

"Sannaig," meaning a sandy place. Another informant states that Glen Sannox means the Glen of the river trout—but you are already half-way up the lane—a lane where brambles grow in profusion in September and early October, and now you are at the gate of the old cemetery, wherein is interred the body of the man Rose, who died under such dramatic circumstances on Goat Fell many years ago. This old burying-ground is all that remains of a chapel dependent on Kilbride Church, and dedicated to St Michael. A rude image of the saint is to be seen upon a stone built into the outside of the wall. The house was probably connected with the Abbey of Kilwinning, which Sir John Monteith, Lord of Arran, granted in 1357, the lands of Sannox and patronage of the Church—*vide* Bryce's *Arran*, page 147.

A little beyond the cemetery, the path follows the light railway track to the Barytes mine, and beyond is just the wild bogland of Glen Sannox. The aspect is wildness personified. All is bleak and stark. The hills on either side rise smoothly to steep heights, but, away at the head of the glen, the sight is one perpetual wrinkle. In all that wildness not a house is to be seen, though at one time the glen rang to the sound of men about their work. The change took place about the time of Waterloo. Formerly the people worked the farms in groups, but now individual tenants took over the farms. It is understood that in North Sannox a little township disappeared, and that, during these years of change, more than 400 people emigrated, chiefly from Sannox.

In this glen is a boulder, known as the Cat Stone or Battle Stone. This word "Cat" seems to be a corruption of a Gaelic word meaning a battle. Various instances arise throughout Scotland of these Battle Craigs—for instance, the Cat Craig in Strathblane, which is supposed to mark the site of a battle fought by the famed King Arthur. This Battle rock in Glen Sannox is supposed to commemorate the slaughter of English soldiers—the hated Sassenach—by the local people. A party of Cromwell's soldiers from Brodick Castle were out collecting stores, or, as the modern soldier has it, "scrounging," and their conduct being resented by the locals, a fight ensued, with the result that the soldiers were killed.

Sannox is the place for adders, but do not be alarmed! Your strong boots are ample protection. For a while you keep by the stream, and then later bear to the left, working gradually through the tangly heather to the Saddle. This is a high ridge dipping down from Cir Mhòr to rise again to the Goat Fell range. Whoever is the leader of the excursion must choose the simplest route and not take any undue risks by tackling the very steep parts. Nearly all the way to the ridge of the Saddle, you will encounter the heather, but once into Glen Rosa, it is conspicuous by its absence. Lunch is usually taken at this vantage point, and, as you munch your sandwiches, you can let your eye rove from peak to peak. Cir Mhòr is near at hand, the key mountain of all the range. You look into the bowl that is the head of Glen Sannox, and raise your eyes to the proud head of Caisteal Abhail, and then, following round to the right, you come to that rocky chimney at Ceum na Caillich, and so to Suidhe Fhearghas, which constitutes the north-western wall of the glen. While you are having lunch, you can watch the deer loping in single file down to the water, and then, after taking their fill, moving off with easy grace to mingle with the heather in the distance. Another spur from Cir Mhòr leads to the Beinn Nuis range, described in another chapter, and still another ridge, the one you are on, leads up to Goat Fell. From this ridge you can look into the Coire nam Fuaran, a corrie surrounded by castles of rock, whose floor is littered with fallen castles. Those who wish can extend the tramp by climbing to Goat Fell summit and then down into Brodick, but for this you should have a competent guide. It is a stiff ridge walk all the way. If you attempt this extension, do not be tempted to descend into Glen Rosa, as this is a very dangerous route, which has cost one life and very unpleasant experiences for others. Descend either to Brodick or Corrie, the former place for preference.

Assuming that the super-strenuous have now started their further ascent, and that you are of the party going to Brodick by way of Glen Rosa, proceed down hill to the stream. Gradually, as you descend, the mountains around Glen Sannox drop out of sight, until presently nothing is seen of the glen you knew all morning. So to the stream and the head of the glen. Here you are on the edge of a wild corrie, rising up to Cir Mhòr and Beinn Tarsuinn and the Ceims ridge connecting the two heights. On the other side of this ridge, the hills slope at a gentler gradient in Glen Iorsa. Across Glen Rosa, you will see the long white streak of a waterfall, which has its source in that high corrie immediately under the summit of Goat Fell.

Once you have reached the glen stream, your route is simple to follow, except that the rough path is particularly boggy, and it is really essential to be careful how you tread. In spite of my watchfulness, I sank up to my thighs in one boggy bit. One foot trod on firm shingle in the bed of a hillside streamlet, but the other foot sank into black oozy, slimy peat. Imagine my state when pulled out, but imagine the worse state if the victim had been a woman.

A feature of the Rosa Burn is the crystal clearness of its waters and the bleached state of the rocks in the stream. The bed of the burn looks as if it had been newly spring-cleaned, while the water has that clean, green tint so good to look upon. In parts the water runs over rippling shallows, and tosses in madcap fashion over small rock formations. In other places, it runs deep and slow, taking upon itself a deeper tinge of green, and gliding along with a quiet movement of dignity, so foreign to its attitude a few minutes ago, when it laughed with glee as it jumped the fall.

Looking back, you see the sharp ridge of the Ceims, which, when séen from a greater distance, is said to bear a striking resemblance to a certain statesman, and was known years ago as Lord Brougham's profile, but to-day the ridge is more popularly referred to as "The Sleeping Warrior." To obtain the best impression of the Sleeping Warrior, it is advisable to climb to some vantage point on the north Ayrshire coast. If you are possessed of a fair share of imagination, you should have no difficulty in shaping the outline. The front of the warrior's helmet (or Lord Brougham's nightcap) is the slope up from the Cir Mhòr Col. The four pinnacles close together may be taken as—first, the peak of the helmet; second, the nose; third, his moustache. Following this is a dip which represents his lower jaw. The long rise to the top of the Castles represents the chest. From the height of the chest, slopes carry the outline down to a ridge representing the topboots, and so down to the imaginary feet.

By now you have reached the junction of the Rosa Burn and the Garbh Allt, and so to the last stage of the tramp to Brodick. Ere leaving the glen, it would be appropriate to refer briefly to the meaning of the word "Rosa." The name is said to mean "Ferry Point," according to Bryce, and his explanation is worth repeating here. "This name 'Ferry-point,' as indicating that water may have filled the glen since men inhabited the island, is remarkable, especially when taken in connection with the anchor found in the glen . . . we cannot assign to a very great antiquity the use of iron anchors, nor a modern origin to the old sea cliff which surrounds Arran, for it could only have been when the sea stood at that old level that Glen Rosa was occupied by the sea . . . it was usual to ship cattle at high water in the Cloy, from a natural pier of stone a little way west of the smithy garden, north of the road." The writer goes on to say that the island must have been raised 25 feet at least to lay dry the Ferry-point Glen. He says the name may refer to a lake, and that the existing mound is very like the remains of an old lake barrier. In a book of local place-names, the definition is given quite differently as the Glen of the Horse.

The sharp division of scenery in Arran is striking. Craggy peaks are congregated in the north end of the island, while the feature of the southern half is rolling uplands. A deer fence divides the hills of the north from the rolling uplands of the south—a fence which keeps the deer to the hills and the "grouse to the moors." The highest point in the southern uplands is 1,492 feet, whereas the mountainous northern half culminates in a height of 2,900 feet—Goat Fell. This "hill of the winds" has a much greater appearance of height than its actual altitude would suggest, possibly because of the fact that it rises from sea level

All of the 2,900 feet belongs to the hill whereas with many other heights, especially abroad, part of the altitude has nothing to do with the actual mountain in question.

It is a pity that Goat Fell is not just a little bit higher, so that it could have qualified to be included in that more select band of heights in Scotland that claim to be over 3,000 feet—"The Munro Tables." This list is given in the "General" Guide Book issued by the Scottish Mountaineering Club. After tea in Brodick motor or walk to Lamlash by the road. If you walk, rest awhile by the head of the road, and look back at that maze of jagged rock formations now standing up in their black cloaks against a purpling sky.

> The lengthening rays of the setting sun
> Gild the heights with cloth of gold,
> While deep in the glens at the foot of the bens
> The shadows creep eerie and cold.

Glen Rosa

E. W. Tattersall

THE CLAUCHLAND HILLS

"But here we will kneel to the wild forest queen
On this green grassy dais that the sunbeams are fleckin'."

Route in Brief.—Clauchland Hills and Corrygills. Route by field paths to Strathwhillan, returning either by highroad or shore. Walking distance, 8 to 9 miles. A pleasant and easy walk, not calling for any heavy hill climbing. However, you will be advised to wear stout brogues.

THE Clauchland Hills divide the Brodick and Lamlash Bays, culminating in the Clauchland Point and the Hamilton Rock. A road cuts over the high ground from Lamlash to Brodick to the west of these hills, while a track can be followed all the way by the shore. A path leads across the hill to Dun Fionn, a grassy height above the point, from Seabank, leading up by Mount Pleasant to the Clauchlands Cottage and Farm. This way is sometimes boggy and marshy, and, to avoid this, you could follow the shore road a little farther and then follow the by-road to Clauchlands Farm and join the path over the hill. A little above the farm reservoir is a path, according to the map, which branches in a westerly direction across the face of the hill to join the Brodick road somewhere in the vicinity of the Isolation Hospital. This path, however, I could not find, and I am doubtful of its existence.

Many and varied are the excursions you can make over these hills or by the shore. One Sunday afternoon, I followed the woodland at the back of Altachorvie (Lamlash) up to the moorland, and so to the ridge, where I sat for a while alternately reading and absorbing the wonderful view of the Brodick Bay and the peaks above.

> " Great wide, beautiful, wonderful world
> With the wonderful water round your curl'd,
> And the wonderful grass upon your breast,
> World, you are beautifully drest."

My favourite spot, however, is the summit of Dun Fionn, that grass-covered old fort that commands such a wonderful vista of sea, mountain and moor. In the mornings, I have watched from these heights the white mist cuddling the shores of Brodick or sailing serenely round Goat Fell. In the afternoon, I have dreamt, and slept, and read on the grassy carpet of the summit. In the evening, I have watched the wonder of a Highland sunset, glowing and then fading behind those grim peaks. I have sat at this old beacon post when the heat haze danced on the waters ; I have stood at this beacon post and leaned into the gale, the while shouting defiance at the elements in a voice that sounded pitifully weak in that volume of rushing wind ; I have danced a jig on Dun Fionn for pure joy of living, when the snow has placed its mantle on the heights and the grass is crisp and white with frost. I would have you know this outpost of the Clauchlands, and, knowing it, hold it dear for all that it may mean. Let me tell you of a night I spent on Dun Fionn, where these notes were written.

Any hilltop will do—provided the night is good. Beforehand, you must prepare so that you are ready to start at the first favourable opportunity. Some there are who set out haphazard for this adventure, but to obtain the utmost enjoyment out of the affair, an endeavour should be made to provide some degree of comfort between the waiting hours of sunset and dawn.

To let you know how I prepared, I will explain my position at present. I am sitting in my hike tent, with the night around me, my only illumination is the candle, stuck on the upturned bottom of my " tinnie." Outside, there are quiet little sounds that ripple through the velvet of the night.

I have pitched my tent in a hollow just below the summit. Behind me is Lamlash Bay, and in front Brodick and its attendant heights. Two hours before sunset, I wandered up the hill, and, while the golden banners of the sky streamed across to the mainland, I gathered my bed of heather for the tent. Then, spreading my ground-sheet, I arranged my one blanket to look like four. Next, I emptied my rucksack and filled it with heather, and so provided myself with a pillow. I wouldn't use the bracken, because of the rather heavy smell it has. Thus prepared, I climbed to the summit to witness the dying day. It had been my idea to write my impressions as I sat, but now I find I cannot. That's all.

Dungoyne offers a wonderful expanse for a sunset, and Earl's Seat for the sunrise. Ben Lomond is a favourite spot, and because of that I have shunned it. Ben Ledi, while it is a good viewpoint, is a bit weird and awesome for a night vigil, especially if one ponders too long on the legend of the Pool of Death—that quiet wee loch of Ben Ledi. Ballageach, with its wide, open spaces, offers scope, and so does the summit of the Stoneymollan Road, Balloch.

For a night on the hills, I leave it to you to choose your hill. To appreciate such an adventure you must be an experienced tramper and a real lover of the hills.

You must be able to enjoy the quiet of hills at night, and not be afraid of the grey stillness of the wide open spaces. Comes a rustling in the grass as the night wind whispers to the lapping waves ; a lamb bleats sleepily, a tree branch creaks—these are some of the sounds that frighten some people, but to others are just part of the scheme of things.

It is also necessary when arranging a night on the hills to be prepared for a sudden change. Clouds gather from nowhere in particular, the wind drops, and the mists come down, bringing the fine rain that soaks so quickly. Recently I was caught on the hills on such a night without a tent. The evening was so fine and warm that I lay down to sleep with no protection beyond a ground-sheet and a blanket. In the dark of the night, I awoke to find myself enveloped in mist and the rain falling.

My resting place was in a hollow of the hills, about 1,200 feet up. The hill and moors seemed to envelop me, and the mist prevented me finding the way down. There was nothing else for it but to wait for the dawn with as much patience as possible.

A little after four in the morning, the intense blackness slowly turned a dark grey, and then by degrees the stunted bushes loomed up like trees in the near distance. In the half-light, I found the path downhill. Through the bracken to the pasture lands, and then to a farmyard, where my nailed boots made an awful clatter on the stones, waking both the echoes and the inhabitants. So eventually I came to the edge of the mountain mist, when the greyness of the dismal day was accentuated.

That ended one night on the hills, and, although not a success, it was an adventure worth having. To wake up in the middle of the night and realise you are all alone on a lonely hillside, with mist swishing all round about, is indeed an adventure just as the tracing of the hill path in the grey dawn was another.

When one is fortunate in witnessing a sunrise, then is the realisation that Nature in all her splendour does not surpass the awakening of the day.

As the black of night is beginning to fade, the birds shake their feathers and ascend to herald the dawn.

The lark "that sings the stars to sleep," rises up to fulfil its mission, the cock awakens the farmyard, and bunny peeps out of his burrow to see what the day will have in store.

Gradually the light increases, and, as the sun draws near to the rim of the world, all is tinged with a rosy pink. The gloaming brought the golden hour, but the dawn brings its delicate tones of pink. Thus heralded, the sun comes over the rim to commence its daily ride across the sky. Its first duty is to chase the mists away from the hilltops and remove the stray clouds lightly resting on the valley woodlands.

The night has gone, day has started on its course and the joy of the sunrise is now a memory—a glorious memory.

But this is not getting on with the job of taking you the excursion I planned.

Leave Lamlash by the Brodick road. Up this hill, you go through an avenue of trees, past the club-house of the golf course, and so on to the moorlands. Climbing steadily, you come to the crest of the road and the wonderful panorama of peaks. I remember on one occasion motoring to Sannox. We left Lamlash in clear, bright sunshine, and, at the summit of this road, looked down on a white sea of billowing mist, which appeared to slide down Goat Fell to settle over Brodick and the shore road. Then descending, we entered this mist, and our view was obscured until we returned again over the hill to

Lamlash, when clear atmosphere was once more encountered.

In October of that year, I had another interesting fog experience. The boat was late in arriving at Lamlash, and word came that fog in the Firth was holding up steamer traffic, and yet Lamlash Bay was entirely clear and bathed in bright sunshine. Outside the Bay, beyond Clauchlands, the white bank of fog blanketed the view, but no mist entered the bay during the whole of that day.

From the summit of the hill, the road leads down through the woodlands to Brodick. At the commencement of the woodlands, you will find a path on the left, which leads down to Brodick, providinga pleasant diversion from the road. Travelling the road all the way may not appeal to you, in which case, you should strike across the moorland on the right, before reaching the summit of the hill. Well away from the road (on the right), you will see the isolation hospital, screened by trees. Keep this on the left, and wander just as the fancy pleases, until you decide to make for Brodick. During the shooting season, it is advisable to watch where you are going, as you may run a considerable risk of being shot, as well as being a nuisance to the shooting tenant.

Brodick Bay is a joy to see and a picture to remember for the dull, dark days of the city in November. To be able to conjure up this vision on a wet winter's day, sitting in a tramcar returning from business, is to be lifted out of your surroundings and be carried away to a place of sun and fresh air. Just as I was carried away when reading about David Grayson and his fun with a tin whistle, so am I carried away by such memories as I hold of Brodick Bay. The beauty of a wide sweeping bay is accentuated by the whiteness of the long stretch of smooth sand, which reaches back to the cool green of the grass. The grass introduces you to the woodlands which drape the hem of the hills. The hills culminate in Goat Fell, the mother of Arran, a mountain which crowns this superb picture of West Highland scenery.

When you have done with Brodick, your return to Lamlash may be made by way of Corriegills and the path between Dun Fionn and Dun Dubh (the black fort). The pathway to Corriegills leads off the Lamlash road up Strathwhillan. For a while, you are near the shore, and then the path climbs up to the forts, but, before describing the view overlooking Lamlash Bay, let me say something about Dun Fionn. From its commanding position, the situation is ideally placed for a fort or beacon station, and it is little wonder, therefore, that tradition tells us that this was Fingal's Fort.

In *East of Arran*, you read that " once upon a time, there were giants in Arran. They say that the chief of the Giants was called Finn or Fingal, and they tell how he and his sons and clansmen hunted wild beasts on the island and did great deeds. The hill above

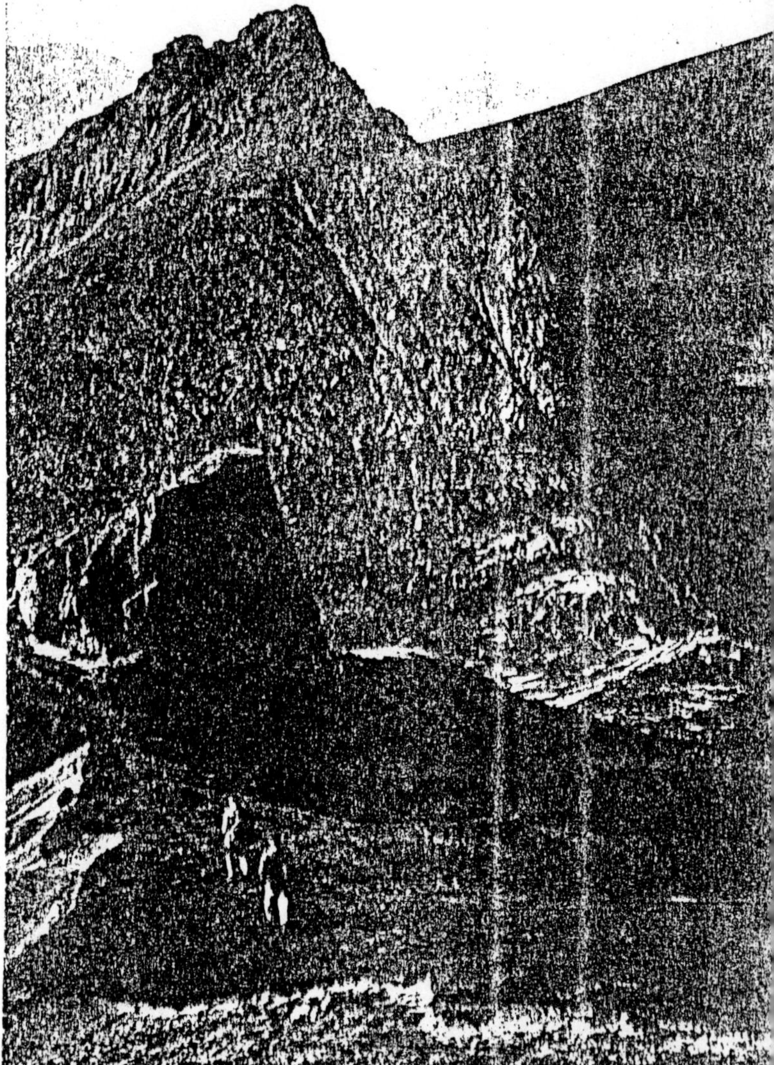

Mighty is Arran—Looking to Cir Mhòr *Andrew C. Gray*

Bennan Caves

E. W. Tattersall

Clauchlands Point, Lamlash, called Dun Fionn, was a fort of his." Next, you read in Bryce's *Arran*, that Dunfion or Fingal's Fort, is the highest point on this portion of the ridge, right over Corriegills shore and 500 to 600 feet in height. A low mound, enclosing an elliptic space, 40 yards by 16, is seen round the summit, but nothing whatever is known of the history of the fort. From traces of vitrifaction, said to have been noticed on the stones of the mound, it has been conjectured that the place was the site of a beacon fire in the wild old times, as well as a stronghold."

As a look-out station, there is no doubt that the position would be ideal, and it is not surprising to read, therefore, that Dun Fionn was one of the island's chief defences. With walls 5 feet in thickness, the place must have been well-nigh impregnable, and would constitute a serious menace to any enemy contemplating an attack on the island.

Treading the corridors of history from the times of Fingal, you come to the exploits of the hardy Norsemen, who cast envious eyes on the comparative civilisation of the island. There is little doubt that it was visited by the Norse rovers in their earlier expeditions, and it is certain that, in later times, these men of the north held the island until they were ousted in the 12th century by Somerled, founder of the great family of Macdonald, Lord of the Isles. In later days, probably Bruce would use this as a look-out station, although Kingscross Point is given as the place where he watched for the beacon fire at Turnberry. In still later days, when Cromwell's men garrisoned Brodick Castle, they may have found this high vantage point of use as a look-out station.

So much then for the historical, but what of the view from the fort? Earlier in the chapter, I described the prospect over Brodick Bay, but now your feet are set towards Lamlash, and, as you breast the hill, the southern aspect opens up. Immediately below is Lamlash Bay, where fleets throughout the ages have found sanctuary. The fleet that fought King Athalstan at the Battle of Brunanburgh gathered here, as did the ships of King Hacon of Norway, who was utterly defeated at Largs by the Scottish King. To-day the King's "Navee" comes in peace each summer to anchor in the bay, when the holiday-making citizens visit the boats and dance with the sailors, both on the ships and in the large hall along the road to Benlister.

"The Bay of Lamlash," says Headrick, "may be about 3 miles in a right line from its northern to its southern entrance; and at its centre, it forms a sort of semi-circle nearly two miles across, having the Holy Island on one side and the vale of Lamlash on the other. The two inlets may be about a quarter of a mile in breadth at their mouths, and widen gradually as they approach the central bay. The southern inlet is preferred by mariners, because here there is no danger but what is seen. The northern inlet is equally safe to those who know it; but the tails of rock we have described as projected from Dun Fionn, and the gradual decrease of altitude of the rocks on the opposite point of the Holy Isle, cause them to extend a considerable way under the sea, before they sink out of the reach of vessels drawing a great depth of water."

The bay of Lamlash is considered one of the best harbours in the Firth of Clyde—if not in the world.

Having taken your fill, descend by the path to Clauchlands Farm, seen below, and so once more to the village, or follow the line of the hill down to Clauchlands Point, and then home by the shore.

THE BEINN NUIS RIDGE WALK

"Who cometh over the hills
Her garments with morning sweet,
The dance of a thousand rills
Making music before her feet."

WHILE reading through the description of this excursion, keep your one-inch to the mile map of Arran spread at your side, following the routes as you read.

This is the tramp I did with five stalwarts one day in May. None of us had been over this route before, and so we were all leaders and all followers. Climbing the hills, the one with the strongest pair of lungs led, and on the steep edges, Blakeney led, for he is the lad for heights. He glories in standing on the edge of a 2,000 feet drop, while we poor mortals crawl up on hands and knees, and only dare poke our nose over the edge.

Seen from certain points on the mainland, the Arran peaks present a striking resemblance to a soldier at rest—a bold, rugged outline that tempts the strenuous strider of hills.

I am not quite sure how much of this soldier's anatomy I have scrambled over, but, in this instance, I will conduct you to the summit of three peaks, finally descending at a point near the warrior's fifth rib (metaphorically speaking).

Be sure that each member of your party has a good head for heights. Although, in the course of this walk, you have no need to walk along the edge of a sheer precipice, some of the gradients are very steep—steep enough for some people to be affected with giddiness.

Commence the tramp from Rosa Bridge at Invercloy, beyond Brodick. Here is the junction of The Corrie Road and The String Road to Machrie Bay. A few yards along this highway, turn to the right by the church, and follow the winding lane towards Glen Rosa.

The mountains are nearer now, and even more impressive, and soon you leave the last whitewashed cottage behind ,and enter the narrow confines of the wild glen. After about a mile of walking, the glen curves round to the right at a point where a stream on the left comes leaping downhill in a series of white cascades.

In places, you witness a mad, roaring leap of tossing waters, and in another stage of the descent, you see the smooth stream slipping down a trough of rock to topple into a convenient pool.

The stream, called the Garbh Allt (the rough burn), is where the real work commences, as you must follow it right up to the corrie below Beinn Nuis. The strength of your lungs will be tested, and the strength of your boots, too. Up and up you go—on the left side of the stream all the time.

Bog and heather and moorland stream—all must be taken in your stride—a slow, steady tread that knows no weariness. As you climb, the view unfolds. First, Brodick Bay and the Clauchland Hills, then the top of the Holy Isle peeps up over the hills, and later the whole of Lamlash Bay is seen.

After the steep climb up by the stream, you come to the tableland and the corrie under Beinn Nuis. You now observe a horseshoe ridge with Beinn Nuis on the left, Beinn Tarsuinn ahead, and Beinn a' Chliabhain on the right. The object is to negotiate this horseshoe, which might well call for the remark that the real work is yet ahead.

If you climbed the shoulder of Beinn Nuis in the same line as we did, you will see a peculiarly shaped rock. It is shaped like a great mushroom, and is no doubt the result of weathering. Perhaps this too was a haunt of the fairies before they left the island. That is, if they really did leave. According to one story that is told in Arran, the fairy folk found the island too "holy" for them and so they crowded on to a fishing vessel leaving for Ireland. The evacuation operation was so popular that the small boat was sadly overloaded, but it was not disclosed whether the boat reached its destination or not. The same story-tellers say too that the springs and burns visited by the fairies were supposed to possess curative properties, and pails of water were carried quite long distances for sick persons.

At the top of the first shoulder, you have an extended view of the south end of the island and the Kilbrannan Sound and Kintyre.

So to the last steep part of the cairn, where you fling yourself down, breathless with the climb and the view. The day we did this tramp was perfect, and the six of us sat enraptured. We all thought we could see Ireland, and it was not all imagination. From this, the first summit, we walked along the ridge up to the summit of Beinn Tarsuinn. Looking north from here, there is a wonderful V-shaped cleft in the mountains, through which you can see Bute and the mainland.

The next stage in this mountain walk is to negotiate the broad curve of the horseshoe to Beinn a' Chliabhain (pronounce it Chilblain—it is so much easier), and here you need a steady nerve and a cool head. The definition of this Gaelic word is given as "The Hill of the Little Cradle." The rock-climber of the party now took charge (before this we all led in turns), and promptly led to a ledge that stepped off into nothingness for 1,800 feet.

The next venture was to emulate a mountain goat, when we successfully followed a sheep track across the screes of the horseshoe, and so, on to "Ben Chilblain." This is quite an easy climb, grass all the way, but at the summit, there is a sheer drop to the bottom of Glen Rosa.

One long, sloping side of the mountain will lead you

in a steady descent to Glen Rosa, and so back to Brodick.

Needless to say, this tramp is only for the strenuous, and can be done in about five or six hours. As a comparison, the ascent of Goat Fell takes two hours from Brodick.

After tea in Brodick, you will feel quite fit to walk through Strathwhillan (the holm of the holly) and over the hill to Lamlash and dinner. If this does not appeal to you, arrange for the motor to pick you up at Woolley's in Brodick. Walking distance for this tramp—three mountains.

A PICNIC RAMBLE.

Some of the rambles I have described should be attempted by heroes only, so, for the benefit of those who wish a lazy day and yet get entirely off the beaten track, let me suggest an easy saunter in Benlister Glen. There is no need to go far, because you soon find yourself at one with the quietness of the hills, where the only noises are from the stream and from your feet as you crush the heather and bracken.

The entrance to Benlister Glen is by the post office in Hamilton Terrace. The road you take branches off to the left, and follows a level course by the Holy Well and the village hall. Tramping along the straight stretch towards the clachan of Benlister, you will see the Letter Wood to the right, up the hill. To the left of this wood is a stream, where watercress grows

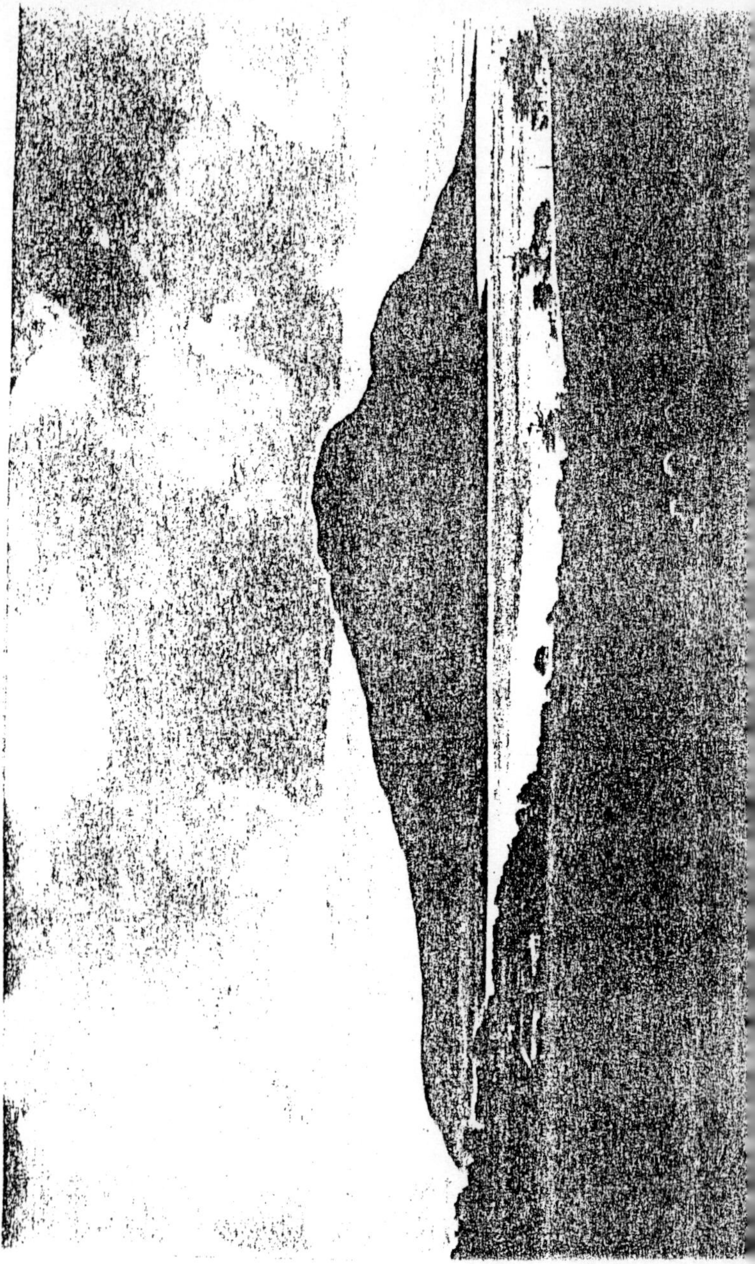

plentifully, and, if you be so minded, you could take home a supply for tea. To be sure of finding the proper place, ask at the house below the wood. The house is called Laigh Letter.

And so to the cluster of whitewashed cottages. The definition of this glen means "the glen of the hill of the vessel"—a culinary vessel.

Here you may wander just as you please, paddling, exploring or sitting at ease, where "Rowan and birch hang couthy together." There is no object in going farther than the junction of the streams. To the left the Benlister Burn winds under the Tounie Hill, to lose itself in the heights by Brisderg. The stream on the right—the Tounie Burn—rises on the slopes of the Sheeans, that hill which looks down on Glen Dubh and Glen Cloy.

If the day is hot, you will find time to sleep, read and ramble to your heart's content, coming home in the earlier evening feeling that—

As I lay me down to rest,
This day has really been the best
Of all that God has lavished on mere man,
For I've watched the bees and smelt the clover
And studied the sweep of the wheeling plover
Stretched flat down to study a flower,
Or flat on my back for a passing hour,
To gaze at the clouds in the deep blue vault—
—If I had not been happy it was nobody's fault.

F

LOCH NA DAVIE

IN connection with the Beinn Nuis walk, you could follow Glen Iorsa from the summit of Beinn Tarsuinn right up to the watershed under Caisteal Abhail (The Castle of Death). Over the watershed, you come to Loch na Davie, under Beinn Bhreac, from which point you follow the stream down through the steep glen, Easan Biorach, to Loch Ranza. Here you would go by motor back to Lamlash.

Two streams rising on Beinn Nuis are called Garbh Allt. One flows to the west to Glen Rosa ; the other flows south to the Machrie Water. From the summit of Beinn Nuis, you command a view of the two streams, so that you should find no difficulty in striking the south-going stream. Follow this down the hill and through the moor, and you will come to the Machrie Water and The String Road, about 5½ miles from Brodick. If you have a compass with you, a pleasant alternative would be to follow in a line due south from the top of Beinn Nuis to the String road. In this way, you would come near the mountain pool, Loch nam Faoileag (The Seagulls Loch) ,and then to the top end of Gleann Easbuig. You could follow the stream down this glen to the road, or, still walking to the south, climb out of the glen and over the hill into Glen Shurig and The String Road, some three miles from Brodick.

THE FALLEN ROCKS

HERE is a plasant walk round the northernmost part of the island : Motor to Sannox Bay and return from Lochranza. This walk does not call for the endurance and stamina of the mountain walks, but, because it is to be a ramble by the seashore, do not be tempted to wear fancy shoes. The way is rough and rocky in parts, and would spoil any but sturdy footwear.

A pathway crosses the stream of North Glen Sannox, and follows by the shore to the Fallen Rocks, a huge agglomeration broken from the cliffs. Here it is pleasant to sit on a sunny day and watch the shipping, and lazily follow with the eye the fat, fleecy clouds that meander in the slender breeze.

I remember, years ago, when staying near Lochranza ,watching the *Davaar* and the *King Edward* racing for the pier. Both were due about the same time, and, although the *King Edward* was faster, the former boat sometimes arrived first. This particular day, the *Davaar* was the first to make the pier, but the skipper of the "*King*" was not to be outdone. He sailed in and berthed alongside the *Davaar*, his passengers disembarking through the first vessel. In this manner; he had the last laugh and was first away.

The walk to the Fallen Rocks is about two miles from Sannox Bay, a distance that will not take up much of the day. You can, if you wish, continue beyond the Fallen Rocks by Millstone Point, right round to the Cock of Arran, a rock having a resemblance at one time to a cock. Beyond this point, you come to Newton Farm and a path to Loch Ranza. Before reaching the Cock of Arran, *i.e.*, at Laggan, another path follows the hill over to the entrance to Glen Chalmadale.

Should you not wish to continue farther than the Fallen Rocks and were minded for more wild, mountainous scenery, you could retrace your steps to North Sannox Bridge, and then follow the road to the next bridge. Here, leave the road, and follow the stream up to the very heart of things. This would be a wild and dirty walk, and if this be your mood for the day, you will find your heart's desire in these glens under Fergus' Seat and The Castles. Do not be tempted to do too much, and check your going by the map. Also, come back the way you went. The impression this district has left on me is one of greatness, gloom and eerieness. Perhaps it is because I last tramped this way as the dusk was falling, on a grey day on my way to Corrie, and motored back in the purple of the darkening twilight. I was not alone then, but on another occasion I walked from Corrie to Loch Ranza alone, and, although the day was bright and sunny, the vista up North Glen Sannox was majestic and solemn.

THE CUDDY DOOK

THOSE who go to Arran during the latter part of September, see the island at its best. The bracken is turning gold, the air is more bracing than at any time during the summer—and the nuts are there for the pulling. Assuming that you can be in Lamlash at this time, you could not do better than arrange a nutting expedition.

The directions are easy, for your destination is Kingscross Point. You can see the sweep of the bay from the house, and can, therefore, quite easily see your route. Going through the village, you leave the road at the Parish Church and follow the shore path to Cordon and on through the wood. This path—the Cuddy Dook—leads up to the Whiting Bay road, but you will take the first path leading down to the shore, and then ramble at your ease, right on to the point. Soon you will come to the hazel trees, where you will see the nuts growing in clusters. The distance to Kingscross Point is most deceptive from the house. You imagine you can easily accomplish the expedition between breakfast and lunch—so you can, but there is little time for gathering nuts. I advise a whole day, and picnic by the shore, and indulge in the fun of making a fire and drinking tea you wouldn't look at, at home.

GLEN ORMIDALE

THOSE of you who know your Arran well, and delight in finding new hills to conquer, will find a tit-bit here that will satisfy you for a day set aside for somewhat less strenuous work.

You will know the Glen Cloy walk and on to Glen Dubh, and so over the hill to Benlister Glen. You should know, because it is such a grand walk, but it is less likely that you will be so well acquainted with Glen Ormidale, that short and wide glen (for its size) branching off Glen Cloy. Many a time have I passed by the mouth of this mountain pocket, but never once have I explored it until recently.

I had the morning free, but there was not sufficient time at my disposal to go off to Goat Fell, or the fine ridge of Beinn Nuis. The morning could not be wasted, so I decided to try the round of Glen Ormidale.

From Brodick you follow the road from the pier going round the bay, and after about a mile you will have passed the village hall and have come to the bridge at the bend in the road where the burn goes singing to the sea. On either side of this bridge there is a road, but you will follow the one on the far side.

A little further on you come to a fence on the right of the lane. This fence hides a beautiful garden which is just visible at one point. In this glimpse you have a vision of gaily-coloured tulips and the fairy blue of the wild hyacinth. The bank by the stream is also gay with flowers. The shy violet peeps out from the grasses; the primrose reflects the sunlight in its gay little flower, and the hyacinth sends forth a delicate fragrance that scents the memory of their glory. The stream goes singing by, murmuring to the flowers and the tree roots, caressing the smooth stones of the river bed, and flashing back the brilliance of the sun at every opportunity.

At the last of the cultivated fields you come into the open glen, when you make your way to the mouth of Glen Ormidale. Follow the stream until well into the glen. When I say follow the stream I do not mean that you use it merely as a guide, but that you walk up the bed of the stream, or that you keep by the bank all the time. You will find such bonny little corners so unexpected and so beautiful. A rocky corner where the stream goes into shadow, and where the overhanging trees bend right down to the water. It is here that I like to scramble through, even though there is quite an easy path round about. Half the fun consists of doing these little daft bits.

When well into the glen leave the stream and start the ascent of the wall of the glen on your left-hand side. It *is* a wall, as you will discover, and yet when viewed from Brodick it does not look the least bit formidable. It provides a nice little bit of scrambling, and, if you like, some good patches of hands and knees work. I am not a man who likes to go climbing with a rope, but I do enjoy the thrill of some hands and knees work.

This hill face will give some good stuff on which to practice—something to provide the preliminary to such places as Cir Mhòr.

Having come to the top, there is nothing of particular interest in the view, but when you get round to the northern wall of the glen you have a grand vista of the peaks in the north end of the island.

In working round the wide curve of the horse-shoe you will cross the hump that is the Black Craig. Between it and the northern wall that is called Muileann Gaoithe there is a gully down which a stream takes a short cut to the floor of the glen. You could have a most enjoyable scramble down this water course, but I would advise you not to miss the walk along the ridge.

You will cross screes and see some splendid and quaint rock formations. Mostly a grey stone, except in one place where there is an outcrop of some soft red-coloured stone.

The way that the rocks have been piled up makes one think that the gods had been having a grand reshuffle of the landscape, and that they had left off in a hurry. This ridge provides the end of a fine walk.

It is easy going, except at the finish, where you have a patch of heather to cross. Later on in the season, when the bracken is high, the hillside will be more difficult to cross, but a small item like that will not deter the real tramper.

THE CASTLES, CIR MHÒR AND GLEN ROSA

Route in Brief.—North Sannox Bridge—North Glen Sannox Burn—The Corrie of the Witch's Step or the Valley of the Stones—Caisteal Abhail (The Castles), 2,817 feet—The Highlanders Well—Cir Mhòr, 2,612 feet—The Comb—Glen Rosa—Brodick. Walking distance, 12 miles and two mountains.

THE starting point is North Glen Sannox on the road to Lochranza. The route on this occasion is the line of the burn leading away to the heart of the glen. The left or south-eastern slope of the glen rises up to Creag Ghlas, which acts as the outpost of the Witch's Step corrie. The north-western side of the glen is dominated by the bulk of Sail an Im. In between, the heather moorlands sweep in a wide curve, at the bottom of which the North Sannox Burn sings its way to the sea. Follow the North Glen Sannox Burn until you come to where the stream forks. To the left the hill stream comes down from the Witch's Step corrie, the other stream has come from the valley of stones or, as I called it, "The valley of desolation." Either way will take you to your objective—The Castles—but the left-hand fork is preferred.

This will lead you up to a point just below the Witch's Step. This is a huge V-shaped cleft of rock on the line of the hill that forms the western wall of Sannox Glen culminating in your objective—The Castles. It is not in the line of your climb to negotiate the Witch's Step, but if you want a thrill, and some right good scrambling, you have it there. Do not attempt anything beyond a mere visit unless you are an experienced hand at rock scrambling, otherwise you may find yourself in a dangerous position which might end fatally. Apart from the personal damage involved, it should also be remembered that others who may have to form a search party, are involved too.

You will follow the stream to its source and then continue in the same line to the summit where you are in the midst of a weird assembly of huge rocks. The view is far and away grander than that from Goat Fell. There is an almost sheer drop down to the basin of Glen Sannox; a high ridge sweeps round to the summit of Cir Mhòr. The massive nature of the mountain is accentuated from this view point and the line of the Saddle and the ridge to Goat Fell stands out sharp and clear.

In due course you will move on and follow the ridge round to Cir Mhòr. Always keep well on the western side of the ridge, on the Glen Iorsa side. In this way you will approach the summit of Cir Mhor from its only accessible side. On all other sides it is steep rock built up in huge slabs. There is room on the alternate summit for one or two only and it is advisable to keep well back from the edge unless you have a good head for heights. Some people are born to walk on ledges like cats, while others must acquire the habit. If you have that fear you must learn to conquer it in your own way. I am all right on almost any height so long as it is not a sheer drop below, or if I have some form of security, such as a rope.

From the summit of Cir Mhòr descend the way you have come and then continue southwards on the Glen Iorsa side of A' Chir (The Comb). Your object now is to climb down The Comb to Glen Rosa, but this looks well-nigh impossible. However, if you watch carefully you will find the break in the ridge where a path leads right down to the Rosa Burn and so back again to Brodick. Do not attempt to negotiate the Comb Ridge, because apart from it being very stiff and dangerous in parts it will lead you to the Beinn Nuis which is another day's excursion.

Here is an alternative to be done as an extension to the Beinn Nuis ridge walk. From the summit of Beinn Tarsuinn, follow the north ridge, known as A' Chir (The Comb), which leads to Cir Mhòr. Be careful to keep on the western slope of The Comb and by no means attempt the eastern side, or you will find yourself in considerable danger. To follow the line of the ridge is impossible. The Glen Rosa side presents a sheer precipice, and the Glen Iorsa side is very steep, and consists of huge smooth slabs that give no foothold. You must, therefore, traverse the Glen Iorsa slope of The Comb below the slabs. An easy ascent can be made of The Great Comb from the west side only, as on the other three sides, sheer precipices drop down to the glens. The summit constitutes a small plateau, where a foothold is secure, but anyone who has not a good head for heights is not advised to scale the slopes to this towering view-point. The view from this height is of the finest, being in the heart of the mountain range, and thus enabling you to pick out the various peaks and work out the line you followed to some of the summits.

Descent, though steep, can be made into Glen Rosa, "the glen of bogs," from the low ridge at the base of Cir Mhòr. This is very steep, but not too hazardous. This provides an alternative route which is preferable to returning the same way. Once in the glen, follow the stream right to Brodick.

THE HILL OF THE BIRDS' NESTS

THE "Trespassers will be prosecuted" sign is unknown on the hills of Arran. Practically the whole of the island belongs to the Duchess of Montrose, who allows free access to both the hills and the moors. It is expected, however, that those tramping over the hills and moors during the shooting season will give a wide berth to any shooting parties they may see. It is a common failing for trampers to want to shout from a hilltop, but during the shooting season in Arran your feelings should be restrained. Whether or not you agree with this type of sport is not the point, the fact remains that you should not interfere with other people's sport, particularly when you are on their ground. You are given the freedom to indulge in your own particular pastime, and in return you should respect their wishes. Another point to remember in Arran is that Glen Iorsa is the breeding ground of the deer and it is the one place in Arran you are asked not to visit. This need not cause you any alarm as you will certainly not wish to visit this particular glen. This statement is not meant in any sense of "sour grapes," as you will realise to the full when you see Glen Iorsa. During this excursion when you come to the "Loch of the two rivers" you look down this bare glen and surely you will agree with me it is not worth visiting.

If you are staying in Brodick it will be necessary to travel by 'bus from Brodick Pier to Loch Ranza Pier, where you should arrange to meet about 9 o'clock in the morning. Incidently, you might suggest to your landlady that a small tin of lettuce be included for the party. Then if you purchase one or two lemonade cubes you will turn your mid-day meal into a feast. The lettuce could be washed in the stream where you rest for lunch and after this has been consumed by the party (the lettuce, not the stream), the tin could be used as a common drinking receptacle. Sandwiches should be cut the same morning and not the night before, and liberally sprinkled with water. It is also advisable to omit meat from the mid-day meal and rely upon jams and fruit for the insides of your sandwiches. Your meat meal can quite well wait until the end of the day.

From Loch Ranza Pier follow the road inland to Glen Chalmadale. On the way you will pass Loch Ranza Castle standing as the guardian at the entrance to this sea loch. At the head of the glen the road bends round to the left and climbs up into Glen Chalmadale, skirting on its way the bulwark of the Hill of Birds' Nests. This hill is your first objective and you would be well to keep to the right of the road until you come to its highest point. From there you can follow the long slope of the hill on your left to bring you to the summit. It is not a long or arduous climb although it is fairly steep in parts.

The summit is only a little over 1,000 feet and as you are over 200 feet at the highest point on the road, you will have only some 800 feet of open hillside to climb.

On the western side of the Hill of Birds' Nests you have a few craggy bits. The best plan is to keep more or less along the ridge at about the 800 foot contour line. Before you depart, however, it is necessary to say something of the view. The whole of the island of Bute will be stretched out for your delight. You will see Rothesay Bay, Loch Fad, and Ettrick Bay, to name only a few of the dominant features of this island. The line of the Kyles of Bute will easily be followed and you will have an extensive view of Loch Fyne. Kintyre will be seen as well as the islands of the sea. You will be fascinated by this view and although you will have had many similar prospects from the different mountains in Arran, each one offers you something new. From the top of this hill you will follow the line of the Glen of the Little Heifer (Gleann Easan Biorach). If as previously mentioned, you keep to the 800 foot contour level you will then only have to climb out at the top end of the Glen. Do not be tempted to follow any of the tributaries. Keep your eye on the mountain stream and follow it right up to the Loch of the Two Rivers (Loch na Davie).

This wee mountain lochan resting more than 1,000 feet above sea level, nestles at the foot of the steep slopes of the Black Crag and Beinn Bhreac. You have followed the stream up to the Loch, but you will notice that another stream flows out of the other end of the Loch which makes its way right down Glen Iorsa. You are standing on what is a very abrupt water-shed. As you stand facing Glen Iorsa, you have Beinn Bhreac on your right. Climb this hill if you wish but failing that, you should skirt the slopes to come to the head waters of the stream tumbling into the Glen called Gleann Diomhan, which in turn joins the Glen of the Wild Cat (Glen Catacol). Follow this stream from its source right down into the lonely Glen Catacol. There is no footpath down this Glen and so you will make your own way. The going will be boggy and muddy, but in due course you will come to Catacol Bay, where the main road will give you a fine two miles of walking to end the excursion.

Catacol Bay is bonny at all times; I have happy recollections of a holiday spent at one of the white-washed cottages in the row that dominates the bay. This row is referred to as the Twelve Apostles. I have never been a great hand at fishing, but I had a number of thrilling experiences in Catacol Bay. On one occasion I thought I must have caught a whale, but on hauling up the line I found I was hauling up the anchor. On another occasion I caught nothing but dogfish, which had to be battered to death as soon as they were caught.

ROUND THE ISLAND

A MOTOR tour round the island is a very good way to spend one of the rest days of your holidays. The route has, of course, been walked by many, but as the normal time for such a walk is three days it seems too large a slice of a holiday to spend in road walking. The marathon walker would do the whole round in one day—in fact, it has been done. Some years ago "marathon hiking" as it was called became well known. Len Clacey did some astonishing feats, including the round of Loch Lomond, in an incredibly short time. Then there was the feat of climbing the three highest peaks in Great Britain in 24 hours—Ben Nevis, Scafell and Snowdon. There is a different kind of record which is popular in and peculiar to Arran. The Arran "regulars" do not boast of having climbed Goat Fell in a certain time. Instead, it is the fashion to put on record the number of times the hill has been climbed. Just what the record is I do not know.

The road distance is 55 miles, and the time taken is 3½ hours.* The usual plan, however, is for a party to charter one or two motors and take the whole day for the trip. The first stop is Blackwater Foot, where a halt for an hour or two is made for lunch, and a walk along the coast to the King's Cave. On again to Loch Ranza, where the afternoon is spent boating, bathing, putting, or rambling. An excursion that can

* See Appendix I., pages 106–107

be done from here is to the Faery Glen. After tea, the final part of the journey is made back to the house. That is the excursion in outline. Now read further and find out what it holds in store. It will not be necessary to describe the entire journey in detail, because parts of the road have come within the scope of previous rambles. From Brodick right round to Drumadoon, the road is not new, although well worth a second visit. The object of this chapter, therefore, will be to describe the way from beyond Drumadoon to Brodick by way of Loch Ranza. The west coast of Arran is not so interesting as the east. Across the Kilbrannan Sound, which divides the island from Kintyre, the hills are not so impressive, nor is the distant panorama to be compared with that from the east: Kilbrannan Sound, however, should hold your interest, as this is the centre of the famed Loch Fyne herring fishery. During the day, you see the fishing boats in their harbour along the coast, and as evening draws on they creep out to their work. Gone are the days of the sailing vessels. All are driven by petrol engines. The boats work in pairs, each boat holding an end of the net. At first spread out, the boats generally close in on one another until they meet, when the net is drawn in and the catch sorted out. Next comes the sale of the fish. The attention of a fish carrier is attracted by a flare which is hoisted by the fishing vessel. Along comes the larger ship, a bargain is struck, the fish transferred and the money paid over on the spot, and the fishing boats, if time permits, prepare for another catch. When, in the very early hours of the morning, these boats return home, the steam drifters (owned by fish dealers) head for Fairlie and Ardrossan on the mainland of Ayrshire, where the boxes of fish are entrained for Glasgow and the markets. Wherever shoals of herring are, there you will see the gannets flying about, gorging themselves on this harvest of the sea. These birds fly at a low altitude but with great speed, and suddenly stop in their flight and drop like a stone into the water coming up again with a fish. It is a sight I never tire of watching, and the amazing speed and dexterity with which they make their catch will always be a source of wonder to me.

After lunching at Drumadoon, you will continue your journey over the moorland to Machrie Bay and the junction of The String Road. There is a tale of the fairies of Machrie Moor. They were in the habit of meeting at Durra-na-each, near Shiskine, and for amusement throw pebbles among the trees of the forest, the rule being that the stones be thrown from between the fingers and thumb. The years have gone by, but still those stones lie there on the moor where a tradition of Fingal still lingers. One of these stones is known as Fingal's Cauldron Seat—Suidhe Choir Fhioin—and was believed to contain a fairy or brownie who could be propitiated, only by the pouring of milk through the hole in the side of the stone. This hole, which is sufficiently large to admit two fingers, runs perpendicularly through the side of the column. Tradition states that to this stone Fingal was wont to tie his favourite dog, Bran.

> "Before the leash was prepared for him,
> Bran, though but a whelp,
> Killed a deer more than each of the rest."

Before reaching Machrie post-office, the road crosses the Machrie Burn, a considerable stream, descending from Glen Ture and falling into the bay to the north of the King's Cave. This river flows through a rocky channel, which, in one part, has worn through a rock, and left so contracted a gap at the top as to form a very easy step across. "Yet not long ago," Pennant tells us, "a poor woman in the attempt, after getting one foot over, was struck with such horror of the tremendous torrent beneath that she remained for some hours in that attitude, not daring to bring her other foot over, till some kind passenger luckily came by and assisted her out of her distress."

Beyond Machrie, the road hugs the rock-bound shore to Dougrie shooting lodge, where you obtain a view of the heights up Glen Iorsa. This glen holds good tramping possibilities. You could motor over The String Road to Machrie and then walk to Dougrie. From this point, you would follow the Iorsa Water to Loch Iorsa, and on to the second tributary on the right, which should be followed up to Loch Nuis. Here you are on the slopes of Beinn Nuis. Make this your objective and then follow the Garbh Allt to Brodick, from which place you could motor home. Making your way up Glen Iorsa, you should have no difficulty in finding your way to Brodick. Follow up the long, sloping east wall of the glen, and when you reach a commanding height looking down on Brodick, map out your route accordingly. If you care to follow the first stream on the left beyond Loch Iorsa, you will climb up the slopes of Sail Chalmadale and come to Loch Tanna. By climbing up and over the heights at the north end of the loch, you will come into the steep and wild Glen Catacol, and so to the clachan of Catacol on the coast road near Loch Ranza.

To continue the motor journey. From Dougrie, you go through the woods and past Imachar Point, where the palm trees grow, and so to Pirnmill, which used to be the last port of call for the Campbeltown boats before crossing to Kintyre. There is no pier at Pirnmill, and the boats used to heave-to in deep water, while passengers and goods were convoyed to and from the shore in a large rowing boat. When the weather was stormy, this operation was far from pleasant. The up-to-date railway time-table will indicate whether Pirnmill is included this season as a port of call.

Beyond Pirnmill, the road sweeps round to Catacol Bay, where a fine view is obtained from the wooded, winding switchback road. The deep indentation of Catacol Bay curves in to the entrance to the Glen, which is guarded by a row of neat, whitewashed cottages (the Twelve Apostles). The serene blue of the waters reflects the glaring whiteness of the cottages, which appear to assume alarming bulges and distortions should the water become agitated.

In M'Arthur's *Antiquities of Arran*, it states that a cairn stood by the shore to commemorate the defeat of Manos, King of Sweden. The tradition states that, after being defeated, Manos was disarmed and bound by Fingal, but was released after promising to return to Sweden, but the promise was not kept and Manos returned again, this time to be killed in battle.

> " So were the mighty overturned
> As they fell under our feet in battle.
> Manos, leader of the host, has fallen
> Like a fiery meteor in the forth of currents."

Many years ago, the stones of the cairn were removed to provide road metal.

And now to Loch Ranza, where you spend the afternoon.

It would not be fair to compare any one part of the island with another, as each holds its own charm. Who would presume to compare Brodick Bay, and, likewise, who would want to make comparisons where Loch Ranza is concerned ? This " loch of Arran's isle " penetrates to the doorstep of the mountains, where the road climbs steeply up Glen Chalmadale.

> " A sea loch's inmost bend
> Is narrowing to its end."

Keeping a watchful eye over loch and mountain,

the old castle of Loch Ranza stands desolate by the water's edge. Nearby the fishing boats find anchorage, but not always a haven, for the storm can lash in fury in this seemingly landlocked bay, yet

> "This castle hath a pleasant seat; the air humbly and sweetly recommends itself unto our gentle senses."

This ruin, once a royal residence, was apparently habitable two centuries ago. First mentioned by Fordun in 1400, it was occupied by Ronald MacAllister in 1445 for a rent of £16, 6s. 8d., and "twelve bolls of bear." The castle and lands were later given by James II. to Alexander, Lord Montgomery, whose grandson was created Earl of Eglinton. In 1685, the property passed to the Montgomeries of Skelmorlie, and eventually into the hands of the Hamiltons. In the description of Loch Ranza, Pennant says, "The approach was magnificent; a fine bay in front, about a mile deep, having a ruined castle near the lower end. The whole is environed with a theatre of mountains; and in the background the serrated crags of Grianan-Athol soar aloft." Lord Teignmouth, speaking of the loch's winter aspect, said, "In point of gloomy grandeur, no British bay excels Loch Ranza." Then we read in the *Lord of the Isles*, Scott's impression—

> "The sun, ere yet he sunk behind
> Ben Ghoil, the 'mountain of the wind,'
> Gave his grim peaks a greeting kind
> and bade Loch Ranza smile."

Within this glen, Bruce's sister lived a lonely life at the convent of St Bride's. No trace of the chapel now remains. After exploring Lochranza, you will continue the last part of your motor excursion up the steep and wild Glen Chalmadale and over the watershed to Corrie and the east coast. This is the route followed by Bruce and his men, after landing on the island; this is the way the old priest came when he delivered the message to Bruce on the eve of sailing for Carrick.

> " His cowl the good old priest did on,
> Took his piked staff and sandall'd shoon
> And, like a palmer bent by eld,
> O'er the moss and moor his journey held.
> . . . . . .
> Heavy and dull the foot of age
> And rugged was the pilgrimage."

The road is far better to-day, but all else is unchanged. Wild the aspect, and mighty to a degree, when the summit of the road and the watershed into North Glen Sannox is reached. The jagged peaks are seen now from a new angle and lose nothing by it.

Passing over the Witches' Brig, where an old witch is said to have disappeared (in the good old days), the road follows on into North Glen Sannox, down which the view is exceptionally fine. So once more to Sannox Bay and old familiar places. On through Corrie and by the shore, where action of the sea through ages has excavated caves in the cliff side. Then the wide, sweeping bay of Brodick comes into view, and, finally, you top the rise to look down on Lamlash.

Many and varied have been the views to-day. At

the south end of the island, wide vistas of sun-kissed ocean, spreading away to a hazy horizon, held our enraptured vision. Then the loneliness of the Machrie Moor and the rural calm and shady woods of the east coast run. Quaint Catacol, a row of whitewashed cottages, and so to the citadel of the north end of the island—Lochranza. Glen Chalmadale introduced you to the mighty mountains that were all amongst you at Sannox, and then, finally, you had the mingling of mountain, moor and sea as you drove for home.

" So comes the evening,
Far remote and retired from the noise of town
I'll exchange my brocade for a plain russet gown.
My friends shall be few
But well chosen and true ;
And sweet recreation our evening shall crown."

APPENDIX I

ARRAN ROADS

Reproduced by permission from Gall & Inglis
"Contour Road Book of Scotland"

Round Arran.

Description.—The road round the island, though narrow in parts, and with sharp turns, is a good road. It commands fine views of the Clyde on a clear day. The road is almost level from Brodick to Sannox, but thereafter has 1 in 10-17 hills over to Lochranza. Thereafter it is almost level for 15 miles to Machrie Bay, after which it is undulating, with short hills of 1 in 10, almost all the way to Brodick.

Measurements.

Brodick,* Pier.									
6¼	Corrie,* Hotel.								
14	7¾	Lochranza,* Hotel.							
20⅝	14⅜	6⅝	Pirnmill.						
27½	21¼	13½	6⅞	Machrie Bay.					
32	25¾	18	11⅜	4½	Blackwaterfoot.*				
39⅛	32⅞	25⅛	18½	11⅝	7⅛	Lagg Inn.*			
48⅛	41⅞	34⅛	27½	20⅝	16⅛	9	Whiting Bay.*		
52½	46¼	38½	31⅞	25	20½	13⅜	4⅜	Lamlash.*	
55⅝	49⅜	41⅝	34⅞	28⅛	23⅝	16½	7½	3⅛	Brodick.*

Notes.—2m., Brodick Castle. Corrie: Glen Sannox. Lochranza: Fairy Dell. There is some rather pretty scenery about Lagg Inn. 44m., Kildonan Castle. Lamlash: Fort, fine view of Holy Island. Brodick: Glen Rosa, Goat Fell, Brodick Castle.

Brodick to Blackwaterfoot.

Description.—The gradient of this, The String Road, mostly 1 in 10 over the hill.

Measurements.

Brodick,* Pier.		
9⅝	Shiskine,* Inn.	
11	1⅜	Blackwaterfoot.*

Hotels or Inns at places marked *.

ROUTE 364. ROUND ARRAN.

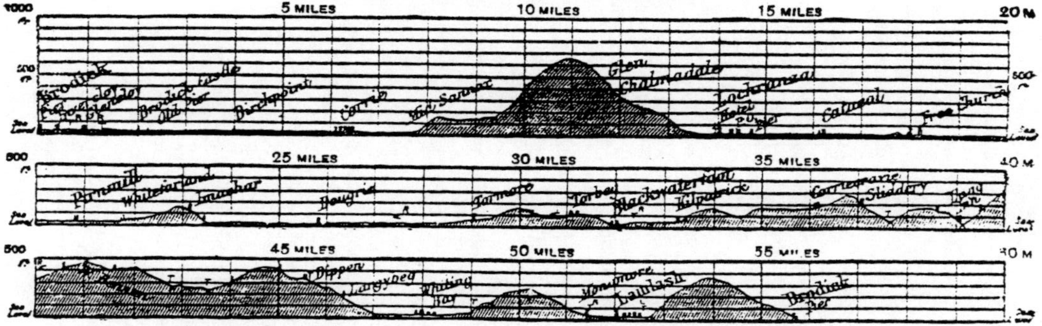

Signs: < Road Fork, forward journey, > ditto reverse, + Cross Roads, ⊥ Road Junction, ∩ Bridge, ⊤ indicates a sharp turn.
The directions R (right) and L (left) for the forward journey are above the Road Line, those of the reverse, below.

APPENDIX II

BOOKS

ALL ABOUT ARRAN. By R. Angus Downie. (Blackie, 1933 2/6.)

THE ISLANDS OF SCOTLAND. Scottish Mountaineering Club Guide.

THE LORD OF THE ISLES. By Sir Walter Scott.

THE BOOK OF ARRAN. Two vols. Issued by the Arran Society.

ARRAN OF THE BENS, THE GLENS AND THE BRAVE. By Mackenzie MacBride, F.S.A. (Scot.); with illustrations in colour by J. Lawton Wingate, F.S.A. (T. N. Foulis, London and Edinburgh, 1911; 7/6.)

THE EAST OF ARRAN. By A. Boyd Scott, M.C., B.D.; illustrated by David Heyland Rudd. (A. Gardiner, Paisley, 1919.)

THE MACBRIDES: A ROMANCE OF ARRAN. By John Sillars. (Wm. Blackwood, 2/-.)

GEOLOGY OF ARRAN AND CLYDESDALE. By James Bryce, M.A., LL.D. (Thomas Murray & Sons, Glasgow; 1865.)

ARRAN. By The Landsboroughs, Father and Son. (Arthur Guthrie, Ardrossan; 1875.)

THE ANTIQUITIES OF ARRAN. By John M'Arthur; illustrated by James Napier, Jun. (Thomas Murray & Son; 1861.)

OUR WESTERN HILLS. By "A Glasgow Pedestrian." (Morison Brothers; 1892.)

SCOTTISH WESTERN HOLIDAY HAUNTS. By T. C. F. Brotchie, F.S.A. (Scot.). (John Menzies & Co., Ltd.; 1911.)

DAYS AT THE COAST. By Hugh Macdonald. (C. L. Wright, Glasgow; 1878.)

POLLOCK'S DICTIONARY OF THE CLYDE. (John Menzies & Co., Ltd., Glasgow; 1888.)

AUTUMNAL RAMBLES AMONG THE SCOTTISH MOUNTAINS. By the Rev. T. Grierson, M.A., Minister of Kirkbean. (James Hogg, Edinburgh; 1851.)

PLACES OF INTEREST IN ARRAN. By Rev. R. Lawson. (4d.)

THE ISLE OF ARRAN AND HOW TO SEE IT. By Rev. David Landsborough, D.D. (1/-.)

ORDNANCE SURVEY MAP OF ARRAN. 1 inch to 1 mile. (Cloth, 3/-; paper, 2/-.)

THE STORY OF ARRAN. By G. Eyre Todd. (1/-.)

THE ISLE OF ARRAN. Illusrrated. (2/6.)

BUCHANAN'S TOURS ROUND ARRAN. (Robert Anderson, Glasgow; 1883.)

THE ISLE OF ARRAN. By Rev. Jeams Headrick. (Constable, Edinburgh; 1807.)

FOUR VIEWS OF ARRAN. By James Ferguson. (J. Menzies, Edinburgh; 1842.)

APPENDIX III

PLACE NAMES

THE meaning of the different place names as given here have been gleaned from the various books (and there are many) dealing with and touching on Arran. Not all the definitions are alike, in which case the two, or three, as the case may be, will be quoted. To go into the matter thoroughly would require a book to itself, and, in consequence, only the barest information can be given.

It is appropriate that such a list of place names should begin with Arran itself. Many are the suggestions :

KIDNEY ISLAND—From the Gaelic "Ara," genitive "Aran," a kidney, on account of the shape of the island.

Dr Cameron, of Brodick, an authority, says this is probably the meaning, and Johnston, in his *Place Names of Scotland*, supports this ; but Currie, in his *Place Names of Arran*, says such a meaning is difficult to sustain.

ISLAND OF MOUNTAINS, derived from "Arr-Inn." (Pennant's definition.)

The following are definitions quoted from Currie's *Place Names of scotland* :

BREAD ISLAND, from Gaelic "Aran"—bread.
FIELD OF FINGAL, from "Ar Fhionn."
LAND OF POINTS, Gaelic "Ar"—land, "Rinn"—points.
LOFTY ISLAND, from "Arainn."
SKY ISLAND, from "Athar Innis."
STAG ISLAND, from "Arr"—a stag, and "Innis"—an island.

This last definition is favoured by Currie, and, in the writer's own opinion, would seem to be feasible. Arran has long been a mountain deer park.

The Norsemen called Arran "Hersey," which also means "Stag Island."

ALTACHORVIE—Burn of the Corrie.
The House by the Burn.

LAMLASH—Formerly the name of the Holy Isle and a corruption of the Gaelic name meaning the island of St Molios. Later the name would be shortened to Lanmolas and so to Lamlash. Johnston says—"Formerly simply Molas; Gaelic 'Lann Lais'—Church of St Las; commonly used in the endearing form Molas or Molios or Molaise." Currie's definition—Eilean Molaisi, Gaelic. This was corrupted into Lan Molaise and, eventually, to Lamlash.

URIE LOCH—Loch of the Brown Water.
Loch of the Yew Trees.

MONAMORE—The Great Moor.

GLEN KILL—Glen of the Kiln.

DUN FIONN—Fingal's Fort.
The Fair Fort.

CLAUCHLANDS—Stoney Land.

BEN LISTER—Hill of the Vessel.
The Arrow Glen.
Penny Land of Alister.

GARBH ALLT—The Rough Burn.

BEINN A CHLIABHAIN—Hill of the Little Cradle.

GLEN SHURIG—Glen of the Colts.
The Shivering Glen.

GLEN SHANT—The Sacred Glen.
The Glen of Storms.

BLAIRMORE—The Great Field.

KILBRIDE—The Cell of St Bridget.

CREAG NA FITHEACH—Rock of the Ravens.

GLEN ORMIDALE—Glen of the Snake River.

A' CHIR—The Comb.

GOATFELL—The Hill of Goats.
The Hill of Winds.

APPENDIX III.

Beinn a' Chasteal—Castle Hill.
Cir Mhòr—The Great Comb.
Caisteal Abhail—The Forked Castle.
The Castle of Death.
The Ptarmigans' Castle.
Suidhe Fhearghas—The Seat of Fergus, son of Fingal.
Cock of Arran—When viewed from the sea, these rocks give the impression of a cock, but the resemblance is not so marked since the head was knocked off.
Glen Chalmadale—The Glen of St Colman.
The Glen of the Reeds and Rushse.
Loch Ranza—The Loch of the Rowan Tree River.
The Loch of Safe Anchorage.
The Loch of Arran's Isle.
Catacol—The Rift of the Wild Cat.
The Vestibule of the Two Nooks.
Ard Bheinn—The Mountain with a Gap.
Beinn Bhreac—The Freckled Mountain.
Glen Rosa—Glen of the Horse River.
The Ferry Glen.
The Red Glen.
The Sheeans—Faery Seats.
Strathwhillan—Holm of the Holly.
Corriegills—A Cauldron or Hollow.
Dell of the Stranger.
Brodick—The Broad Bay.
Glen Sannox—Glen of the Sandy Bay.
Glen of the River Trout.
Cordon—The Little Weir.
Gortonalister—Alexander's Cornfield.
Beinn Tarsuinn—The Traverse Mountain.
Bennecarrigan—The Rocky Hill.
Ceum na Caillich—The Witch's Step.
Cioch na h-Oighe—The Maiden's Paps.
Dippin—The Twopenny Glen.
Dougrie—The Black Rocks or Weir.
Drumadoon—The Ridge of the Fortified Hill.
Glen Iorsa—The Retired Glen.
Pladda—The Flat Island.
Shiskine—Fertility or Moorish Ground.
Sliddery—The Sluggish Water.
Torr Nead an Eoin—The Hill of Birds' Nests.
Sail Chalmadale—The Heel of St Colman.

APPENDIX III.

BEINN NUIS—The Hill of the Fawns.
LOCH NAM FAOILEAG—Loch of the Sea Gulls.
CNOC NA FOLA—The Meadow of Blood.
ALLT A CHRUITEIR—Glen of the Harper.
ALLT NA DRIS—The Blackberry Glen.
CNOCAN AN TUBHA—The Raspberry Hill.
TORMORE—The Great Bleaching Green.
CNOC NA DAIL—The Hill of the Beetles.
SHEDOG—The Windy Place.
DRUIMIGHHINAR—The Ridge of the Gluttons.
ALLT GILLE GHAGAITH—The Burn of the Stuttering Lad.
BEALACH GAOTHAR—The Windy Gap.
SLIABH MEURON—Faery Thimble Moor.
CNOC NAN CAM HAIRLIE—Consultation Hill.
KISCADALE—Coffin Dale.
KINGSCROSS OR PENNYCROCE—Crossing of the King.
COIRE NAN LARACH—The Hollow of the Mares.
SAIL AN IM—The Hill of the Butter.
CORLOCH—Loch of the Cranes.
ALLT NAM BROIGHLEAG—The Bilberry Glen.
NARACHAN—The Place of Snakes.
GLEANN EASAN BIORACH—The Glen of the Little Waterfall of the Heifer.
MADADH LOUNIE—The Wolf's Lair.
ALLT NA COLMAN—The Glen of the Pigeon.
MIALL NAN DAIMH—The Stag Hill.
ALLT MADADH DHUINN—The Otter Glen.
CNOC BREAC GAMHAINN—The Hill of the Spotted Calf.
CNOC NAN SGITHEACH—The Hill of Thorns.